Integrating the Arts and Humanities into STEM

An Epistolary Exploration – Seeing Through the Clouds of STEAM

Or
Without Critical Reading and Resistance you are Doomed to Become Lost
in Art's Romantic Mist – aka STEAM

Integrating the Arts and Humanities into STEM

An Epistolary Exploration – Seeing Through the Clouds of STEAM

Or
Without Critical Reading and Resistance you are Doomed to Become Lost
in Art's Romantic Mist – aka STEAM

by

Paul T Kidd

Cheshire Henbury

First published in 2020 by Cheshire Henbury.
Paperback version ISBN 978-1-901864-27-4

British Library Cataloguing in Publication Data: A catalogue record for this book is available from the British Library.

Email – Use Email Contact: www.cheshirehenbury.com/emailcontact.html
Web site: www.cheshirehenbury.com/integrating-the-arts-and-humanities-into-stem

Dedicated to the memory of the English poet, painter and printmaker William Blake (1757-1827), whose illuminated books – a juxtaposition of words spoken in silence and the language that has no words – provide inspiration and demonstrate that art does not have to be a slave of the *totalitarians in our midst*, whether these be religious, political, artistic or scientific. Thus do we invite you to hear, once again, the words that we speak in silence, and to see with your mind that which sits in the wordless world that we have conjured to appear along side our words. It is like melody and harmony …

Also by Paul T Kidd

Scriptovisual Works
STARTS Weaving the Art-Science Tangled Web: An Artistic Study of DG
    CONNECT's Adoption of Totalitarian Art Pioneering the Path to
    Europe's Undemocratic Future Past
366 – A Scriptovisual Composition Unknown: An Artistic Investigation of
    the Spaces between Spaces in the Quest to create a post-European Era,
    post-Enlightenment Science
STARTS – Science, Technology and the Arts: The Artistic Voices that DG
    CONNECT Silenced

Fiction
Moments in Time
Enigma
A Tale of Two Deserts: Enigmatic Christmas Fables for the Modern Age
Encounter with a Wise Man: A Christmas Tale of Wisdom
Father Christmas Adventures: Unexpected Tales of Christmas Magic
A Father Christmas Story: Being a Tale of How Father Christmas Came to
    Be

Non-fiction
E-Business Strategy: Case Studies, Benefits and Implementation
Electronic Business: The Executive Guide
Rapid Prototyping for Competitive Advantage: Technologies, Applications
    and Implementation for Market Success
Revolutionising New Product Development: A Blueprint for Success in the
    Global Automotive Industry
Agile Manufacturing: Forging New Frontiers

Edited Books
European Visions for the Knowledge Age: A Quest for New Horizons in
    the Information Society
E-business: Key Issues, Applications and Technologies
Business and Work in the Information Society: New Technologies and
    Applications
Technologies for the Information Society: Developments and
    Opportunities
Electronic Commerce: Opening up New Opportunities for Business
Advances in Information Technologies: The Business Challenge
Advances in Agile Manufacturing: Integrating Technology, Organisation
    and People
Organization, People and Technology in European Manufacturing

PREFACE

This book has a serious purpose and a serious message, but you will have to discover for yourself what these are! You will be much richer, emotionally, spiritually and intellectually as a result. Matters are presented the way they are for a reason. It is called art!

Paul T Kidd PhD, CEng, FIMechE, FIET, SMIEEE

1 October 2020

"Turning and turning in the widening gyre
The falcon cannot hear the falconer;
Things fall apart; the centre cannot hold;
Mere anarchy is loosed upon the world,
The blood-dimmed tide is loosed, and everywhere
The ceremony of innocence is drowned;
The best lack all conviction, while the worst
Are full of passionate intensity."
W.B Yeats

The Argument

Heaven and Hell cannot be integrated. Marriages sometimes are convenient, an arrangement that suits. There can be no Heaven without Hell, and no Hell without Heaven. One thing presupposes the existence of the other. Aesthetics can be found in all sorts of activities and there is no one-best aesthetic. To establish something by argument, the premises have to be assumed to be true. The premises define the conditions under which conclusions are true. Premises can sometimes be gross, so gross that it is better to say so at the start. But to do so, alerts the reader to the existence of aspects of reality that have been left-out or distorted, as necessity demands, and then it becomes clear that the premises are self-evidently false. In the world of the objective, things can be other than they seem. In the world of the subjective, everything is as it seems and seems as it is. Life is about assumptions, interpretations and intentions, which find their way by human hand into texts. But those who read the *silent narratives,* who can see, *literary contrails,* they might a different vision have, and in seeing thus, perceive something else. In the light there is darkness, and in the darkness there is light. In the music there is silence, and in the silence there is music. Emergence prevails. Reality is socially constructed. There is no single reality invariant across individuals, nations, and cultures. History is rewritten to suit the needs of the present. Knowledge is that which is believed to be true. Truth becomes what people want to believe is true. Grand overarching narratives are a thing of the past. Increasingly it seems, people dwell in the past. There are a lot of STEM professionals doing this, along with their artists in residence too. This is an inconvenient truth!

Unexpected Item in Bagging Area – Emily Dickinson Gives a Poetry Reading

And now a poetry reading – it is Emily Dickinson reading *Tell all the Truth but tell it slant*. Reading …

> "Tell all the Truth but tell it slant —
> Success in Circuit lies
> Too bright for our infirm Delight
> The Truth's superb surprise
> As Lightning to the Children eased
> With explanation kind
> The Truth must dazzle gradually
> Or every man be blind —"

The Bertolt Brecht Gardening Show

You, the reader, will now experience the Bertolt Brecht Gardening Show. This week, Brecht is interviewing the author of the work that you are now reading. What are you doing? Just reading this, or doing more than reading?

Bertolt Brecht: "Welcome to the Bertolt Brecht Gardening Show! This week our guest is the person who wrote the book that you are now reading, so that's the person who wrote the words that I just spoke. Paul! Welcome!"

Paul: "Nice to be here!"

Bertolt Brecht: "So Paul, we are seeing a growing interest in integrated gardening. And you wrote a book about it. This book in fact. Why?"

Paul: "If I may, I would like to answer your question by comparing an English Garden with a Japanese one!"

Bertolt Brecht: "English! Surely you mean British?"

Paul: "No I mean English. To outsiders, we may all seem to be the same, but there are differences between the English, Welsh, Scottish and Northern Irish people. These differences lead to slightly different gardens, not least because the climatic conditions vary so much. Cultures are different too. My original intention, to compare English and Japanese gardens, will illustrate these points."

Bertolt Brecht: "I am in your hands – literally!"

Paul: "Indeed you are."

Bertolt Brecht: "But why am I saying what I say?"

Paul: "I'm being Brechtian!"

Bertolt Brecht: "I get that. Do you, dear reader? But what about these gardens Paul?"

Paul: "Yes. If you compare a traditional English garden with a traditional Japanese garden, you will discover that they are both very formal and highly structured. Great care is taken to ensure that they remain neat and tidy. But look more closely and you will see some important differences."

Bertolt Brecht: "You are right. But what are these differences and why do they exist?"

Paul: "To explain that I will deal with the matter of nature, and in particular mosses."

Bertolt Brecht: "Let me interrupt you there. I have received a text message from one of our viewers – someone reading this book – who asks why are we talking about integration of gardens? Would you like to respond to this Paul? "

Paul: "I will respond. We are having this discussion because so many other people are doing the same, but in doing so, are talking from the perspective of vested interests. It's surprising how much nonsense is talked by people who want something – usually it's money. People suffering from an excess of rationality are also very prone to talking nonsense. These rational people want to integrate gardens that are so different, but without any understanding about how or why such a thing is possible. It seems to me that this is just people saying something without taking any account of the reality of experience and such people are demonstrating poor standards of thought. In effect, they are saying what they want to say, thinking what they want to think, and finding what they want to find by way of support. That's the answer to the viewer's question. Now back to mosses!"

Bertolt Brecht: "Yes back to mosses!"

Paul: "It rains quite a lot in Japan. It rains quite a lot in the United Kingdom too! The west side of England is renowned for its rain, particularly in the north-western parts, north and south of Manchester. It is said that the cotton industry developed in this part of the country because the air is damp which helps with the spinning of cotton as the threads are less inclined to break than in drier parts of the England. Myth perhaps? In reality there may have been be a number of factors at play which led to the growth of the industry around Manchester. But let's keep things simple and stick with the myth! It saves having to think slowly!"

Bertolt Brecht: "Myth. Let's not forget about myths. It's an important part of knowledge, even for the seekers of objective truth. They have their own myths!"

Paul: "Yes indeed they do, especially about gardens! So do artists, both about themselves and about the seekers of objective truth. The latter are highly inclined to believe these artist's myths as well. Saves having to think slowly and to engage in deep learning, so to speak!"

Bertolt Brecht: "Mosses!"

Paul: "So what ties Japanese gardens to English gardens? "

Bertolt Brecht: "I would say that it is rain and mosses. "

Paul: "Right, but you are supposed to be interviewing me!"

Bertolt Brecht: "I was, but somehow we seemed to have exchanged roles!"

Paul: "I'll continue then as the interviewee and note a difference in thinking between the Japanese attitudes to mosses and the English one. In both situations mosses are a natural feature because of the dampness of the climate. But the Japanese make mosses a feature of their gardens, here in England, mosses are treated as an invading species, spoiling what we have created. So we tend to wage war on them, using chemicals to destroy the moss, or removing it from rocks, grass and soil as much as possible. We keep it under control, and we do not let it take-over. But the Japanese embrace mosses, work with them, turning mosses into a feature of their gardens. "

Bertolt Brecht: "So in one case, gardeners seek to control and overpower nature, while in the other, gardeners work with nature."

Paul: "Yes, and I think that speaks volumes about the two cultures. In Japan, their gardens are spiritual, and have been shaped by their belief systems – Buddhism, Daoism, and Shinto."

Bertolt Brecht: "While English gardens are influenced by the country's Abrahamic heritage and, to some extent, by the Enlightenment?"

Paul: "Yes, and its colonial past, since many of the plants in an English garden have been bred from those originally collected by plant hunters in the nineteenth-century."

Bertolt Brecht: "So to sum up, the aesthetics of Japanese and English gardens are very different."

Paul: "Very different."

Bertolt Brecht: "And can they be integrated?"

Paul: "What does integration mean?"

Bertolt Brecht: "Brought together, the components linked to create a whole?"

Paul: "What assumptions are hiding behind your statement? And why would you want to do such a thing, to integrate the product of two very different cultures, which address two very different realities? Gardens and gardening ideas evolve with time. Let them do so. They're organic."

Bertolt Brecht: "And your garden? "

Paul: "It's unique to me. It's a continuing work of design, development, experimentation, re-design, change, serendipity, and it's a place with a purpose, just like nature has a purpose, and the purpose of my garden is nature's purpose."

Bertolt Brecht: "Thank you Paul for that interesting insight. Perhaps we will be hearing more about integrated gardening in future episodes of the Bertolt Brecht Gardening Show. Thank you for watching (reading?). Until the next time – don't forget to keep gardening! Good night!"

Unexpected Item in Bagging Area – A Japanese Maple Leaf?

A Japanese maple leaf? Or an image of a Japanese maple leaf? Or a silhouette image of a Japanese maple leaf? Or a silhouette image of a Japanese maple leaf collected from a Japanese garden? Or a silhouette scanned image of a Japanese maple leaf collected from a Japanese garden? Or a silhouette scanned image of a Japanese maple leaf collected from a Japanese garden in England? Or a silhouette scanned image of a Japanese maple leaf collected from the Japanese garden in Tatton Park, Cheshire, England?

In the beginning ...

It is not what you know that is important,

Nor even what you do not know.

What will get you into trouble, is what you do not know
you do not know.

or

There is Knowledge of Knowledge,

Knowledge of Ignorance, and

Ignorance of Ignorance.

Misinformation is everywhere ...

Across all ages, in all societies, under every regime
imaginable, there has always been misinformation.
Today is no different from any other era. It can be
found in newspapers, in TV programmes, in books, on
the radio, on the world-wide-web, in the classroom, on
social networks, in the workplace, on the street, in
films, in history lessons, in science, in reports, in ... all
walks-of-life, in all activities. No media, no profession,
no activity is immune. It's there, whether you are
aware of it or not.

Some of this misinformation is intentional, some accidental,
some the product of embellishment, some the result of
ignorance, some the result of incompetence, some an
outcome of ideology, some the result of
misunderstanding, some a consequence of misguided
simplification, some the outcome of myth making, some
the product of romanticising the past. Some is the
result of corruption! Some is a consequence of rampant
and unjustified relativism. Some is the result of biased
research by people who should know better ...

Increasingly we are finding that the product of research is
being corrupted. This is known as the *Research
Integrity Crisis*. We will probably mention this again.

Never in Human History ...

Never in human history has there been a greater need to question and challenge what people and organisations with authority are saying – people and organisations who speak with the voice of authority, either by virtue of claimed knowledge or because of their standing in society.

One reason for this need is that corruption, once again, is becoming the norm: Ka-Ching, Ka-Ching, Ka-Ching! And the lust for power and influence is spreading!

Increasingly too, vested interest groups, often masquerading as being independent, are advising in their own interests. And in the modern world there is a lot of advising to be done!

We are also experiencing a scientific reduction to ignorance.

This is the moment to speak out and to warn, otherwise history will become the future – once again.

A Scientific Reduction to Ignorance

What do the following statements all have in common?

"William Whewell in his 1840 synthesis, The Philosophy of the Inductive Sciences was the first to speak of consilience, literally a jumping together of knowledge by the linking of facts and fact-based theory across disciplines to create a common groundwork of explanation."

"It is bizarre how very little of twentieth-century science has been assimilated into twentieth-century art."

"In 1959 C.P. Snow, the molecular physicist who later became a novelist, declared that Western intellectual life is divided into two cultures: that of the sciences, which are concerned with the physical nature of the universe, and that of the humanities – literature and art – which are concerned with the nature of human experience."

"Any sound scientific theory, whether of time or of any other concept, should in my opinion be based on the most workable philosophy of science: the positivist approach put forward by Karl Popper and others."

"To have art as an ingredient in the knowledge creation and programme development process is a new idea."

A Scientific Reduction to Ignorance

The answer to the question is: All the statements were
made by STEM people and all the statements are
either wrong or highly inaccurate to the point of being
misleading. And yet STEM people are increasing their
power to shape policies, and are manipulating their way
into positions of influence. And where one sees this at
its most advanced stage of development, is in the City
of the Golden Stars, in an organisation that is not
accountable to anyone. And the names are, if you are
interested:

- Edward O. Wilson

- C. P. Snow

- Eric R. Kandel

- Stephen Hawkins

- A European Commission DG CONNECT
  Technocrat.

So when we say that misinformation is everywhere, we are
highlighting a growing problem with people in
authority, as well as a more general problem!

Nissan Admits Falsifying Emissions Tests

On July 9th 2018, the BBC News Web Site reported that Nissan in Japan had uncovered falsified data from car emissions tests at most of its Japanese factories.

The firm revealed that emissions and fuel economy tests had deviated from the prescribed testing environment.

The carmaker added that inspection reports had been based on altered measurement values.

So when we say that misinformation is everywhere, we are highlighting a growing problem with people in authority, as well as a more general problem!

FCC Found to have Implied False Cyber-attack during Net Neutrality Repeal

On June 6th 2018, the IET in London reported that the US Federal Communications Commission (FCC) deliberately fed journalists misleading information about an incident during the public consultation for the net neutrality regulations repeal.

The FCC nudged journalists to report the failure of its comment filing system was due to a cyber-attack rather than due to a mass of net neutrality activists flocking to the site to leave comments defending the regulations.

So when we say that misinformation is everywhere, we are highlighting a growing problem with people in authority, as well as a more general problem!

European Commission Claims that Online Disinformation is on the Rise and is Harmful to EU Citizens

On April 26th 2018, a European Commission press release reported that Online Disinformation is on the rise and that it is harmful to society and to EU Citizens. They offered no evidence to support these claims.

Instead they published a report by experts, who did not question these claims, or offer any evidence to support them, but instead engaged in an authoritarian discourse, while making rather vague and ambiguous reference to human rights and freedom of speech.

So when we say that misinformation is everywhere, we are highlighting a growing problem with people in authority, as well as a more general problem! Or perhaps in this case it is disinformation rather than misinformation!

TED* Too!

On the *TEDx Talks Channel*, from 2017, a talk (from a US arts-based person (an art-science lover?) with 20 years experience as an educator), entitled *Beauty Will Save the World*, in which the speaker says:

"The Nobel Prize winner, the Russian author Aleksandr Solzhenitsyn, wrote in his Nobel Prize acceptance lecture, that 'beauty will save the world'. He was actually quoting Tolstoy from War and Peace."

The *TEXx* speaker then goes on to say:

"Aleksandr Solzhenitsyn won his Nobel Prize for Literature for a book called the *Gulag Archipelago*, and in that he talked about his time spent in the Soviet Gulag system. He was imprisoned because he was an intellectual. He was told that he was a danger to the State, he was a danger to his nation. But what was really happening was that the people in power feared his creativity, and they feared his intellectualism."

Oh really! Perhaps you should fact check these statements! No need, we did it for you ...

TED* Too!

Aleksandr Solzhenitsyn won the Nobel Prize for Literature in 1970. His book *Gulag Archipelago* was published in Russian in 1973 and in English in 1974. The existence of *Gulag Archipelago* was revealed in his Nobel lecture. The text of this lecture was smuggled out of the Soviet Union and published by the Nobel Organisation in 1972.

Solzhenitsyn won the Nobel Prize for Literature for the reason stated on the Nobel Prize organisation web site: "for the ethical force with which he has pursued the indispensable traditions of Russian literature." He accepted the prize in absentia. He did however attend an award ceremony in 1974 after he had been expelled from the Soviet Union and stripped of his Soviet citizenship.

Attempts by the Soviet Authorities to seize and destroy the manuscript of *Gulag Archipelago*, once they had became aware of it, were (self-evidently) unsuccessful.

The text of Solzhenitsyn's Nobel lecture does mention *beauty will save the world*, but the text also states the phrase comes from Dostoyevski. The lecture does not however name the specific work where the phrase can be found.

TED Too!*

The phrase *beauty will save the world* can be found in Dostoyevski's novel *The Idiot*. Here is the extract:

"[...] Is it true, prince, that you once declared that 'beauty would save the world?' Great heaven! the prince says that beauty saves the world; and I declare that he only has such playful ideas as that because he's in love. Gentlemen, the prince is in love. I guessed it the moment he came in. Don't blush, prince; you make me sorry for you. What beauty saves the world? Colia told me that you are a zealous Christian; is it so? Colia says you call yourself a Christian. [...]"

Note that the wording varies slightly with the translation. Here it is: *beauty saves the world*. Sometimes it is: *the world will be saved by beauty*. Sometimes it is: *beauty will save the world*.

The novel is about the depiction of an absolutely wonderful – perfect – Christ like person, referred to as the *Idiot* in the title, and his interactions with worldly, flawed, people.

TED* Too!

About Solzhenitsyn's arrest and imprisonment, he was detained in East Prussia in February 1945 while fighting the Nazis. He was a captain in the Red Army.

In his own words: "I was arrested on the basis of censored extracts from my correspondence with a school friend in 1944-5, basically for disrespectful remarks about Stalin, although we referred to him by a pseudonym. Material complementing the 'accusation' was rough drafts of stories and reflections found in my map case. Nevertheless, this was not sufficient for a 'trial,' and in June 1945 I was 'convicted' by a procedure that was then widespread – in my absence, by a decision of OSO (an NKVD Special Tribunal) – and sentenced to eight years in a labour camp (at that time this was considered a mitigated sentence). Following a month-long holdover at the end of my eight-year term, there came – without a new sentence and even without a 'decree by the OSO' – an administrative decision not to free me but to send me to perpetual exile in Kokterek (southern Kazakhstan). This was not something specially meted out to me but a measure widely used at that time. From March 1953 to June 1956, I served this exile until release from it. Then I returned to European Russia and worked as a teacher while at the same time, secretly writing."

HM Treasury Too!

In May 2016 HM Treasury published a report, entitled *HM Treasury Analysis: The Immediate Economic Impact of Leaving the EU. Presented to Parliament by the Chancellor of the Exchequer by Command of Her Majesty.*

The report focused on the immediate economic impact of a vote to leave the EU and the two years following such a decision.

It predicted that a vote to leave would represent an immediate and profound shock to the UK economy. That shock would push the economy into a recession and lead to an increase in unemployment of around 500,000, GDP would be 3.6% smaller, average real wages would be lower, inflation higher, sterling weaker, house prices would be hit and public borrowing would rise compared with a vote to remain.

It also said that the findings sat within the range of what was described as the overwhelming weight of published estimates for this short-term impact.

HM Treasury Too!

The report also presented a downside scenario, finding that the shock could be much more profound, meaning the effect on the economy would be worse still. The rise in uncertainty could be amplified, the volatility in financial markets more tumultuous, and the extent of the impact to living standards more acute. In this severe scenario, GDP would be 6% smaller, there would be a deeper recession, and the number of people made unemployed would rise by around 800,000 compared with a vote to remain. The hit to wages, inflation, house prices and borrowing would be larger. There is a credible risk that this more acute scenario could materialise.

An expert – a leading UK economist and a former Deputy Governor of the Bank of England – undertook a review of the analysis and is quoted in the report saying that it: "provides reasonable estimates of the likely size of the short-term impact of a vote to leave on the UK economy."

There was an effect, the pound did fall in value, but there was no recession and the economy and employment continued to grow, albeit at a slower rate. House prices did not collapse. Exports actually became more competitive. So the question is this: why were so many experts (who agreed with the report) so wrong? Perhaps an answer follows in due course!

HM Treasury Too!

This is what the BBC News Web Site had to say (in April 2019) about the economic impact of the vote to leave the EU:

"David Cameron, his Chancellor George Osborne and many other senior figures who wanted to stay in the EU predicted an immediate economic crisis if the UK voted to leave and it is true that the pound slumped the day after the referendum – and is currently about 10% down against the dollar, and 10%–15% down against the euro. Predictions of immediate doom were wrong, with the UK economy estimated to have grown 1.8% in 2016, second only to Germany's 1.9% among the world's G7 leading industrialised nations. The UK economy continued to grow at almost the same rate in 2017 but slowed to 1.4% in 2018, the slowest rate since 2012. Inflation rose after June 2016, reaching a five-year high of 3.1% in November 2017. However it has since eased, to stand at 1.8%. Unemployment has continued to fall, to stand at a 43-year low of 3.9%. Annual house price increases have steadily fallen from 8.2% in June 2016 to 0.6% in the year to February 2019, according to official ONS figures."

Unexpected Item in Bagging Area – Art Does Not Foster Scientific Success

On 23rd November 1981 the BBC transmitted a recorded interview with the Nobel prizing winning theoretical physicist Richard Feynman. The interview was part of the Horizon series of science programmes. The programme was called *The Pleasure of Finding Things Out*.

In the interview, Feynman expressed his views on the Humanities! What now follows is an enlightening transcript taken from the programme, which is also a (hidden) narrative on Enlightenment, at least as it is practiced in the relatively closed world of physics:

"I've also been rather one-sided about the science and when I was younger I concentrated almost all my effort on it. I didn't have time to learn and I didn't have much patience with what's called the humanities, even though, in the university there were humanities that you HAD to take. I tried my best to avoid, somehow to learn anything and to work on it. It's only afterwards, when I had gotten older and I'm more relaxed, that I have spread out a little bit and I've learned to draw and read a little bit, but I'm really still a very one-sided person and don't know a great deal. I have a limit[ed] intelligence and I've used it in a particular direction."

Later in the interview Feynman demonstrates his limited knowledge (some might say his ignorance!) when he says:

"Because of the success of science there is a kind of … I think a kind of pseudoscience that … Social Science is an example of a science that is not a science. They don't do scientific … They follow the forms … You gather data, you do so and so and so forth, but they don't get any laws, they haven't found out anything, they haven't got anywhere … yet maybe someday they will, but it's not very developed."

Thus we observe: the fox knows many things, but the hedgehog knows one big thing!

The National Academies Too!

In 2018 the National Academies published a report entitled *Collaborations of Consequence*. In it they say that there are multiple examples of collaborations ranging from American painter Abbot Thayer's invention of camouflage to composer George Antheil and actress Hedy Lamarr's collaboration that led to the invention of frequency hopping – the encryption technology on cell phones that helps to prevent messages from being intercepted.

Sorry but here is some bad news – Hedy Lamarr and George Antheil did not invent frequency-hopping!

Examine the history of the development of spread-spectrum communications and you will find frequency-hopping cropping up several times over the period from the late nineteenth-century to 1940, one notable example being the 1932 US Patent, filed in 1929 by W. Broertjes from The Netherlands, *Method of Maintaining Secrecy in The Transmission of Wireless Telegraphic Messages*:

"Method for the wireless transmission of telegraphic messages by means of Morse or other code, wherein the dots and dashes of which the message is composed are transmitted by means of a plurality of working frequencies which are interchanged at will during the transmission of the message."

Aka frequency-hopping!

The National Academies Too!

Markey (aka Lamarr) and Antheil's 1942 US Patent (filed in 1941) for a Secret Communication System mentions as one application, the remote control of torpedoes using radio signals. It proposes using frequency-hopping to achieve the claimed secrecy. The difference between the two patents (Broertjes' and Markey's), lies in the mechanisms used to achieve frequency-hopping.

In a 1984 article in Spectrum magazine on the topic of Cryptology and the Origins of Spread Spectrum, David Kahn (designated in the article as a Historian of Cryptology) mentions the Lamarr-Antheil patent, noting that the motivation was torpedo radio-control and that "Curiously no secrecy order was placed on it."

A possible reason why the patent was never made Classified is that it is a fantasy invention – it would never have worked, because it was totally impractical. But you need an engineering mind to see that and some basic application domain knowledge, which is evidently lacking in the Patent.

The so-called invention might have something to do with Markey's desire to distance herself from the Nazis and their anti-Semitism given that she was an Austrian national working in Hollywood, and her former husband owned an armaments business that was of interest to the Nazis. Perhaps it was her way of saying: I'm not a Nazi!

What is the Difference between a Parliamentary Democracy and a Technocratic/Bureaucratic State run by Unaccountable Experts?

The answer to the above question lies in the response of the UK Parliament to so-called Fake News and Disinformation, and the European Parliament's response.

The European Parliament asked the European Commission to investigate the matter, who then invited experts to work, behind closed doors. These people did not collect evidence, but instead delivered what they were asked to deliver, confirming the belief that EU citizens have to be protected from disinformation through authoritarian measures, which is what the European Commission was always going to do, because that is the mentality in the City of the Golden Stars and because the EU is not a Parliamentary Democracy, but a Totally Organised society run by Institutions that mirror the Institutions that formed the government of the USSR. It seems that very few people have noticed this! We suggest you check for yourself ... Obviously there are differences!

What is the Difference between a Parliamentary Democracy and a Technocratic/Bureaucratic State run by Unaccountable Experts?

In the UK, a Parliamentary Select Committee investigated, seeking evidence from all sources in an open way, and then came to some preliminary conclusions that it is, democracy that needs to be protected from specific threats that the evidence shows exists. These matters will be widely discussed and debated, leading to ... The work is still on going, but could be draft legislation that protects democracy from activities that the evidence identifies as needing to be addressed – particularly activities by hostile agencies. Then the scrutiny and the modification of the draft legislation begins ...

Fortunately the UK won't any more be subject to the results of the actions of a regime run by unaccountable experts. There are sound reasons why the UK (eventually!) departed from the EU at 11pm London time on January 31st 2020. Reasons that cannot be openly discussed You cannot warn European Union Nationalists of the consequences of their ideology. Everything will be fine – they believe!

What did the UK Parliamentarians Discover that the European Commission's Unaccountable Experts did not?

Comparing the two reports, the one produced by the House of Commons Select Committee on Digital, Culture, Media and Sport, and the European Commission's Experts (summoned to produce a report by the European Commissioner no less)?

This: that the primary problem is the use of so-called computational propaganda using for example such things as social media bots, which originate from external hostile powers intent on influencing people in Western democracies, particularly during elections.

If you look at the report produced by the European Commission's experts, there is no reference to this at all – not even a reference to bots! Like we said, misinformation comes in many forms and is even found in places where the topic is disinformation!

How could it be that so many so-called experts were so ignorant, while the elected representatives of the people (who do not have backgrounds in STEM fields) were so well informed?

Misinformation is ...

Misinformation is everywhere and one of the main offenders are people in authority: scientist, engineers, artists, European Commission technocrats, government agencies, experts ... The list is quite long. And people are worried about fake news! I'm afraid you have taken your eye off the ball, as they say.
And what happens when you do that?

History Records What Happens

"Learn to think and judge for yourself, responsibly. Don't accept everything without criticism and as absolutely true. The biggest mistake of my life was that I believed everything faithfully which came from the top, and I didn't dare to have the least bit of doubt about the truth of that which was presented to me."

SS-Obersturmbannführer Rudolf Höss
(Commandant of the Auschwitz extermination camp,
writing shortly before his execution
for crimes against humanity)

Unaccountable Power Advising Unaccountable Power

Only in the City of the Golden Stars can such madness happen:

The tale of the former (unaccountable) chief scientific advisor (to a former (unaccountable)) President of the European Commission, who speaking of best evidence (whatever that means) demanded that scientists have a seat in government, the case for which was never supported with evidence – best or otherwise!

Perhaps though she was motivated by her correct observation that any 'crack-pot' idea, regardless of evidence for or against, can be pursued in the City of the Golden Stars, because the relationship that the European Commission has with people that they call experts is a corrupt relationship.

STARTS demonstrates the point. So does the notion of the authoritarian reaction that emerged from the City of the Golden Stars in response the so-called damaging problem of online disinformation that experts were unable to correctly diagnose.

Ka-Ching!

"Can you hear it ring

It makes you want to sing

It's such a beautiful thing, ka-ching!

Lots of diamond rings

The happiness it brings

You'll live like a king

With lots of money and things"

Songwriters: Robert John Lange / Shania Twain

Artists too, are now busy Advising and Advocating ...

Artists are busy these days, advising and advocating,

And in the process, towards false claims are inclinating.

It seems they are a wanting now, some STEM funding,

There not being, enough public money for arts funding.

We are not exaggerating!

So they have joined the rest, and are now fully participating in advising and advocating ... in their own interest!

Misinformation is Everywhere. In the Arts Too!
Which might soon bring us to a Report which can
be Described (Primarily) as Artists' Advocating. It's
formal title is:

The Integration of the Humanities and
Arts with Sciences, Engineering, and
Medicine in Higher Education
Branches from the Same Tree

For brevity, when we encounter this
report again, which we will, we will call it
The Integration Report.

In Case You do not Know ...

STEM STARTS to STEAM

STEM: Science, Technology, Engineering and Mathematics

STARTS: Science, Technology and the ARTS

STEAM: Science, Technology, Engineering, Art and Mathematics

Just to confuse matters, STEM in the United States also includes certain social sciences, because the National Science Foundation funds some of the more scientifically oriented social sciences. Whereas in the United Kingdom, these are supported by the Economic and Social Research Council.

In Case You do not Know ...

Integrated Teaching and Integrated Learning

Now you are going to encounter dualities – much loved by Europeans!

Integrated teaching: rather than teaching in a fragmented way around specific classroom topics, these topics are addressed together in a specific context. This approach is sometimes referred to as a teacher-centred approach. Thus people talk about ...

Integrated learning: An integrated approach that allows learners to explore, gather, process, refine and present information about topics they want to investigate without the constraints imposed by traditional subject barriers. It is supposed to be student-centred.

(Note that definitions vary)

See the duality: teacher-centred or student-centred. Implied also, is another duality: passive learning or active learning. Time to move beyond dualities – Ancient Greeks in the City of the Golden Stars will struggle!

Unexpected Item in Bagging Area – Art Fosters War Crimes and Crimes against Humanity

At the heart of the Reich, the following artists, architects, and art lovers:

Adolf Hitler: Aspired in his youth to be an artist, and is also known for his deep personal interest in determining the type of art that was suitable for his New World Order – committed suicide, 30th April 1945.

Joseph Goebbels: Aspired in his youth to be an author and playwright. He is also known for his use of art for propaganda – committed suicide, 1st May 1945.

Hermann Göring: Supreme commander of the Luftwaffe and art collector. He is also known as the world's most notorious art thief. Convicted Nazi war criminal – committed suicide, 15th October 1946.

Alfred Rosenberg: Studied architecture at university and worked for a time in the studio of Estonian painter Ants Laikmaa. He is also known as the Nazi Party's chief racial theorist. Convicted Nazi war criminal – hanged 16th October 1946.

Albert Speer: An architect by profession and the Nazi Party's chief architect. He is also known for his role as the Reich Minister of Armaments and War Production in which he was responsible for the use of slave labour. Convicted Nazi war criminal – imprisoned for twenty-years, died of natural causes, 1st September 1981.

And a lot more too, supporting the criminal regime in what can, at best, be called astonishing errors of judgement. Or was it careerism and opportunism? Whatever it was, it certainly demanded that the artists involved suspend all critical thinking, just like they do today, when they enthusiastically and blindly embrace anything associated with European Unionism! And the names of some who supported Hitler's Reich are:

- Paul Troost – architect

- Leni Riefenstahl – dancer, actress, film director, producer, screenwriter, author

- Heinrich Hoffmann – photographer
- Arno Breker – sculptor
- Josef Thorak – sculptor
- Adolf Ziegler – painter
- Elk Eber – painter
- Hubert Lanzinger – painter
- Adolf Wissel – painter
- Wilhelm Sauter – painter
- Georg Lebrecht – painter
- Ferdinand Staeger – painter
- Karl Diebitsch – sculptor
- Hanns Johst – poet and playwright
- Josef Magnus Wehner – writer and playwright
- Richard Euringer – writer
- Erwin Guido Kolbenheyer – novelist, poet and playwright.
- And many more …

In Case You do not Know ...

Differentiation

Differentiation is another way of looking at the learning issue:

Differentiation is all about differences among learners – how they learn, learning preferences and individual interests. Therefore differentiation is an organised, yet flexible way of proactively adjusting teaching and learning methods to accommodate each learner's learning needs and preferences in order to achieve that person's maximum growth as a learner. It is not about doing less or more, it is about doing the same thing in different ways for different learners – although not everything has to be differentiated.

In Case You do not Know ...

Integrated Approaches ...

These are often suited to Primary School Education because
at this stage in General Education, children do not
usually encounter specialist subject teachers, but a class
teacher who teaches all the material. Some exceptions
can be noted – e.g. music teaching.

In the UK, those with children in Primary Schools may
have noticed that teaching around themes is evident,
which address a range of subjects.

STEAM is a specific method that makes use of the arts in
integrated approaches, mostly in Primary Schools – in
the United States. South Korea is experimenting with
the approach too.

Artists though are not needed in order to adopt integrated
approaches.

But, going beyond Primary, into Secondary and, most
especially, into Tertiary education of professionals, is a
big step. Not one to be taken lightly. Perhaps you think
that artists are qualified to take these steps?

We suggest that you examine The Integration Report for
discussion about these steps. Note the result of such an
exercise!

In Case You do not Know ...

Two Adjectives Unalike in Meaning

From the Online Oxford English Dictionary:

- *Original: Not dependent on other people's ideas; inventive or novel.*

- *Creative: Relating to or involving the use of the imagination or original ideas to create something*

Much work undertaken in STEM research fields is original but not especially so. Likewise for artists and the product of their work. Both groups follow fads, inhabit crowded halls, and join grazing herds. Much research and art, is of little consequence, and both are at times done for the wrong reasons. In this sense art and science are indeed alike!

Margaret Bowden, a psychologist who has researched creativity in the arts, noted in her book Creativity and Art, that the commonest form of creativity is Exploratory Creativity, where people just explore an established field. Transformative Creativity, when artists invent something radically new, is rare.

John Berger noted in his book Ways of Seeing, that: "In no other culture is the difference between the masterpiece and the average work so large as in the tradition of the oil painting." One day some future critic may say the same about that which now comes forth from the art-science lovers' symbolic universe. We just did ...

41

In Case You do not Know ...

Two Nouns Unalike in Meaning

From the Online Oxford English Dictionary:

- *Correlation: A quantity measuring the extent of the interdependence of variable quantities.*

- *Understanding: The ability to understand something; comprehension.*

You can analyse data and discover correlations. You can also analyse the degree of the correlation, which might in fact be so small as to be unimportant. You can also analyse data and discover correlations when no correlations exist.

What correlation does not do however, is provide you with understanding. You might find correlations, but the correlations between two or more things does not mean that there is a causal relationship between them, as there may be other factors at play, which you do not know exist. This is why observations can be so misleading and why independent, repeated, randomised controlled studies are often needed.

Be Careful What You Find in Your Data — You Need to Know This!

A report in the August 2018 edition of *IEEE Spectrum Magazine* dealing with *Making Medical AI Trustworthy*, covered the problem with correlation.

Microsoft's principal researcher Rich Caruana reported an issue that arose with a data set of pneumonia patients, and the training of a machine learning model that distinguishes between high-risk patients who should be admitted to hospital, and low-risk patients who can safely stay at home.

The model correctly predicted that people with heart disease were less likely to die of pneumonia, and based on this, classed them as low-risk, which they were not.

The problem was that the data did not include a crucial piece of information: heart disease patients are high-risk and are therefore admitted to hospital when they have pneumonia, and therefore have a good survival rate! Thus the data was misleading and gave the wrong results.

So be careful what you find in your data! Understanding is more important than correlation.

In Case You do not Know ...

Two Verbs Unalike in Meaning

From the Online Oxford English Dictionary:

- *Integrate: Combine (one thing) with another to form a whole.*

- *Synthesise: Make (something) by synthesis.*

Note the difference. Integrate is mid seventeenth-century: from Latin integrat - 'made whole'. Synthesise derives from synthesis, a noun, which means the combination of components or elements to form a connected whole. Synthesis is early 17th century: via Latin from Greek sunthesis, from suntithenai 'place together'.

Disciplines are a product of synthesis not integration. They are composed by people. They are also emergent, responding to interactions with the world. Complex processes are at work, whereby people create the disciplines they inhabit, but at the same time, the disciplines create the people who inhabit them, which makes them more than just text-book knowledge, theories, concepts, methods, tool, etc. And all is subject to change, to new synthesis.

In Case You do not Know ...

Two Nouns with Future Meaning

From the Online Oxford English Dictionary:

— *Polemic: A strong verbal or written attack on someone or something.*

— *Rhetoric: The art of effective or persuasive speaking or writing, especially the exploitation of figures of speech and other compositional techniques.*

You will encounter these two words later, which is why we introduce them now.

In Case You do not Know ...

280 – 0

280 The number of times the phrase 'critical thinking' is mentioned in *The Integration Report.*

0 The number of instances in which critical thinking is evident in the text that is *The Integration Report.*

Understand?

In Case You do not Know ...

The Integration Report

The study brief was to examine the evidence behind the assertion that educational programs that mutually integrate learning experiences in the humanities and arts with science, technology, engineering, math, and medicine (STEMM) lead to improved educational and career outcomes for undergraduate and graduate students.

In reality The Integration Report is not about the above, for humanities subjects, unlike arts subjects, are barley mentioned. The report is yet another artists' advocacy document, founded on a learned assumption that artists are special people and have magical powers. The report is a product of a hunt for proof of value of using artist, rather than an enquiry into what has actually taken place and the results produced, in the context of ... integrated learning.

So what is the report really about? We will answer in due time ...

You will probably know the children's story with the title: The Emperor's New Clothes ...

In the Emperor's Court – the EC – STARTS a Story ...

Not, in the past, but in the here and now, there is an Emperor who, in his court, the Emperor's Court – the EC – does dwell. Being monstrously fond of his image, he spends other people's money on research, to make himself look smart. He doesn't care too much about anything else. Everything he does is designed to show off his research. He funds research into all sorts of things and is always holding meetings, where people – experts – are found advising. So frequent are such meetings, that when he is holding council with these experts who are advising, people say "The Emperor is in his meeting room, with his experts advising". In the great city where he lives – the City of the Golden Stars that is – life is very pleasant, one of the consequences of having much money, and lots of strangers come there every day – that's another consequence of having much money as well. One day there arrived two artists who started doing some advising, and much advocating!

That Which STARTS to STEAM ...

That which STARTS to STEAM are but socially constructed realities, operating at the level of mythology, which if you care to look – critically – you will find are case studies that:

1. Demonstrate that the predicted consequences of the Research Integrity crisis have now become a reality and that no-one should unquestioningly believe what experts are saying.

2. Make obvious the failings of technocracy.

3. Illustrate that people are retreating into a (mythical) past.

4. Demonstrate that people in the world of STEM do not know how to work across disciplinary boundaries – the boundaries between STEM on one side and the social sciences and humanities on the other. Neither do artists!

5. Disprove their own rhetoric.

Warnings From the Art World – 1

"At some time in the mid-sixties ad hoc committees within the art world were being formed to sponsor art and technology. I was immediately elated: my creative needs might be recognised and fulfilled. Then, just as quickly, I was discouraged by obtuse, confused, or empty attitudes that developed among people of influence. Excitement grew over projects that were formulated with bandwagon haste around this subject. As a fad that came and went, along with so many others of that decade, the art-technology boom left in its wake as much prejudice as enlightenment."

John Whitney, 1980

"Over the years I have been a developer for new technology companies, consultant to NSF research projects, and artist-in-residence at research centres. My own art works have often focused on emerging technologies still in their formative stages. The involvements have been judged valuable by me and my collaborators; yet it is often difficult to trace concrete results."

Stephen Wilson, 2000

Warnings from the Art World – 2

"The danger is that people who call themselves artists, but who are far from excellent, look at business as a new opportunity for making 'fast' money. This could cause a lot of damage. Lack of professionalism is the Achilles Heal of artistic interventions."

Lotte Darsø, 2004

"As regards the practices of cultural agencies, there is a tendency to entangle evaluation, or even research, with advocacy, with the result that there is a hunt for proof of value, rather than an honest enquiry into what has taken place and the results produced."

François Matarasso, 2005

Warnings from the Art World – 3

"I am not saying that people always purposefully lie in evaluation reports, but rather the system as a whole relies on accountability at the expense of real change. I want to ask what the repercussions are of continuously providing dubious evaluation reports. Giving the funders what they want in evaluation reports seems to be another way of showing support for that system. This seems an unusual game to play when those applying for and spending public money may fundamentally disagree with the systems that have made the money available in the first place."

Anonymous, 2008

Warnings from the Art World – 4

"It is a very dangerous thing to assert that artists can encourage scientists to make a leap forward in creativity. That is rhetoric, rather than reality."

Wellcome Trust SciArt Evaluation Report, 2009

"A minority of artists and arts producers who considered themselves to be working at the more critical and controversial end of arts practice believed that the Trust occupied quite a conservative position in relation to mainstream science and that this made it more risk-averse as an arts funder than organisations that were more independent of the science sector, such as Arts Council England."

Wellcome Trust SciArt Evaluation Report, 2009

Warnings from the Art World – 5

"How are we to evaluate PhD projects that present a
wonderful work of art or music or a beautifully
designed artefact in a PhD thesis that presents false
truth claims, inaccurate facts or demonstrably
inapplicable research methods?"

Ken Friedman and Jack Ox, 2017

"The PhD in art and design raises many questions. Much
of the debate so far has been less than informative,
especially in contexts where one group or another
deliberately excludes well-informed experts to ensure
that the debate concludes with ill-informed but
predetermined answers."

Ken Friedman and Jack Ox, 2017

Unexpected Item in Bagging Area – The Hedgehog and the Fox

Isaiah Berlin will now speak:

"There is a line among the fragments of the Greek poet Archilochus which says: 'The fox knows many things, but the hedgehog knows one big thing.' Scholars have differed about the correct interpretation of these dark words, which may mean no more than that the fox, for all his cunning, is defeated by the hedgehog's one defence. But, taken figuratively, the words can be made to yield a sense in which they mark one of the deepest differences which divide writers and thinkers, and, it may be, human beings in general. For there exists a great chasm between those, on one side, who relate everything to a single central vision, one system, less or more coherent or articulate, in terms of which they understand, think and feel – a single, universal, organising principle in terms of which alone all that they are and say has significance – and, on the other side, those who pursue many ends, often unrelated and even contradictory, connected, if at all, only in some de facto way, for some psychological or physiological cause, related to no moral or aesthetic principle. These last lead lives, perform acts and entertain ideas that are centrifugal rather than centripetal; their thought is scattered or diffused, moving on many levels, seizing upon the essence of a vast variety of experiences and objects for what they are in themselves, without, consciously or unconsciously, seeking to fit them into, or exclude them from, any one unchanging, all-embracing, sometimes self-contradictory and incomplete, at times fanatical, unitary inner vision. The first kind of intellectual and artistic personality belongs to the hedgehogs, the second to the foxes."

Monism: one.

Pluralism: many.

There are two types of people in the world: Those that classify people into two types, and those that do not. Nevertheless 'hedgehog or fox' is a useful distinction so long as one does not behave like a hedgehog!

Warnings from the Social Science World – 1

"We observe a striking discrepancy between what participants in artistic interventions value from the experience, and the types of impacts policymakers or managers without experience in the area expect evaluation studies to document."

       Ariane Berthoin Antal and Anka Strau , 2016

"We document how projects were accompanied by attempts to commodify creativity by packaging it as an exchange between the artist's creativity and the company's money or space. However, our analysis shows that such attempts are bound to fail because creativity escapes commodification."

       Elena Raviola and Claudia Schnugg, 2016

Warnings from the Social Science World – 2

"Researchers steeped in critical management theory have not yet participated in the conversation. Such colleagues would certainly challenge many of the current assumptions about the dynamics of artistic interventions, leading to new questions and different interpretations about what is happening when people, practices and products from the world of the arts enter the world of the organisation."

Ariane Berthoin Antal , Jill Woodilla and Ula Johansson Sköldberg, 2016

"It is problematic to assume that the sole purpose of artistic interventions is to improve the existing order of things."

Ariane Berthoin Antal , Jill Woodilla and Ula Johansson Sköldberg, 2016

Warnings from the Social Science World – 3

"Management and management scholars have become so enamoured of notions from the art-world, like beauty, authenticity and passion, and have absorbed them in their language in such a way as to mask the fundamental differences between the worlds. By assuming a high correspondence between 'new' management and the arts, they have blunted the critical voice inherent in the arts that society needs to hear in order to challenge comfortable assumptions and deeply engrained power structures."

> *Ariane Berthoin Antal, Jill Woodilla and Ola Johansson Sköldberg, 2016*

"Most of the empirical evidence tends to be anecdotal on the basis of practitioners' practices with a great emphasis on the positive experiences that employees report."

> *Giovanni Schiuma and Daniela Carlucci, 2016*

The Trouble with Anecdotal Evidence – You need to know this!

Anecdotal: (of an account) not necessarily true or reliable, because it is based on personal accounts rather than facts or research.

The history of medicine is full of treatments, the efficacy of which were supported by anecdotal evidence: blood letting; eating radium; exposure to radiation; electric shocks; voluntary lobotomy; drinking urine; drinking sulphuric acid; drinking mercury and silver, snake oil, ... All supported by anecdotal evidence.

The world of the arts and their engagement with industry and education is full of tales of cures, effects, benefits, gains, etc. that are all supported by anecdotal evidence.

To be consistent, if you believe these artistic anecdotal tales, you will want to be bled, to the drink mercury, to eat radium, to have your brain lanced, etc. as soon as possible to gain the obvious benefits! Go on! Get on with it! What are you waiting for?

Warnings from the Social Science World – 4

"The small but growing body of literature has done more to describe the potential contribution of artistic interventions to a wide variety of outcomes for organizations than to evaluate its actual effects. Much of this literature makes highly compelling arguments based largely on personal experience and anecdotal evidence rather than the systematic study and critical review of actual interventions and their impacts. The anecdotal form of much of the evidence, and the general, often vague statements still make it difficult to distinguish between the effects that have really occurred and those which people would like to see occur."

Ariane Berthoin Antal, 2009

Unexpected Item in Bagging Area – William Blake Gives a Poetry Reading

And now an honoured guest, a man of visions, of strange word articulations, of reverberations across time, of prophetic poems, of a knowing lying far beyond those who in admitted and glorified ignorance are dwelling. William Blake is reading from *Jerusalem: The Emanation of the Giant Albion*. Reading …

"And Hand & Hyle rooted into Jerusalem by a fibre
Of strong revenge, & Scofeld Vegetated by Reuben's Gate
In every Nation of the Earth, till the Twelve Sons of Albion
Enrooted into every Nation: a mighty Polypus growing
From Albion over the whole Earth: such is my awful Vision.

"I see the Four-fold Man. The Humanity in deadly sleep,
And its fallen Emanation. The Spectre & its cruel Shadow.
I see the Past, Present & Future, existing all at once
Before me; O Divine Spirit sustain me on thy wings!
That I may awake Albion from his long & cold repose.
For Bacon & Newton sheath'd in dismal steel their terrors hang
Like iron scourges over Albion. Reasonings like vast Serpents
Infold around my limbs, bruising my minute articulations.

"I turn my eyes to the Schools & Universities of Europe,
And there behold the Loom of Locke, whose Woof rages dire
Wash'd by the Water-wheels of Newton: black the cloth
In heavy wreathes folds over every Nation: cruel Works
Of many Wheels I view, wheel without wheel, with cogs tyrannic
Moving by compulsion each other: not as those in Eden, which
Wheel within Wheel in freedom revolve in harmony & peace."

Warnings from the Science World

"Some of them [artists] were absolute fakes."

Richard Feynman

(Theoretical Physicist & Nobel Laureate),

writing in his 1985 book:

Surely You're Joking Mr Feynman!

Warnings from History

The attitude of technocrats in the European Commission (DG CONNECT) concerning art: Art is useless. It is made useful – given a utility - by intrumentalising artists to work with uncreative technologists and entrepreneurs, turning art into a means of developing unconventional and compelling products, and by using art to "induce changes in individual and social behaviour."

Compare this grubby understanding, the product of instrumental reason which knows no consequences, to Aleksandr Solzhenitsyn's understanding of art and literature: "The sole substitute for an experience which we have not ourselves lived through is art and literature."

Why did he say this? Because, he said: "Art and literature can save an entire nation from a redundant, or an erroneous or even a destructive course." This is quite apt given that what the European Commission's DG CONNECT are doing is exactly what Stalin and Hitler did with art, even to the point of mimicking what Hitler said in 1938 about the role of art!

In the Emperor's Court – the EC – ENDS a Story

So the Emperor walked in the procession under a beautiful canopy, and everybody in the streets and at the windows said: 'Lord! How splendid is the Emperor's new research initiative, STARTS. Nobody wanted to be detected seeing nothing: that would mean that he was no good at his job, or that he was very stupid. None of the Emperor's previous research initiatives had ever been such a success. And he was pleased as Punch with himself. He had no doubt now about his manifest destiny.

Then a little child spoke, saying, 'But STARTS is completely empty. It's just make-believe! Anecdotal stories promoting quack science and technology.'

Strangely, no one took any notice of the child, except one person, who just happened to be standing next to the child, someone who was a social scientist.

"Do not be surprised little one," the social scientist began, "this is how people behave. We have developed many concepts and theories that help in the understanding of this behaviour. Should I name some of these for you?"

Oh yes please," the little child said, not seeking to hide his excitement.

"Very well then. I shall begin ... "

For the Understanding of that which STARTS to STEAM, to the Social Sciences and Humanities

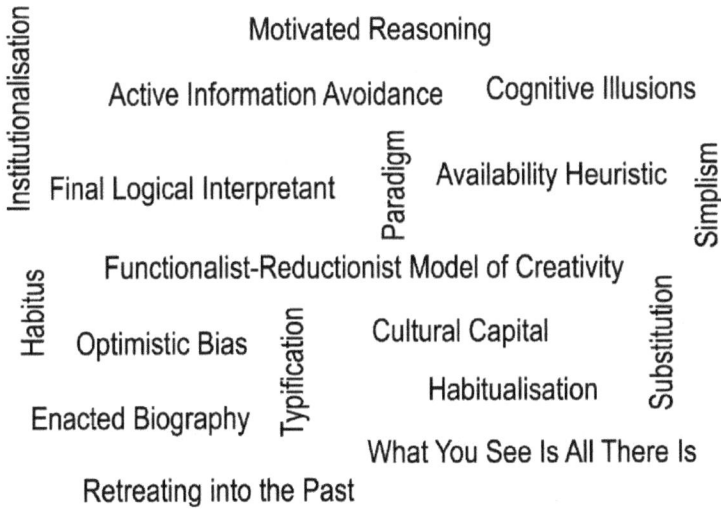

Turn – 1

Motivated Reasoning

Active Information Avoidance   Cognitive Illusions

Final Logical Interpretant   Availability Heuristic

Institutionalisation

Paradigm

Simplism

Functionalist-Reductionist Model of Creativity

Habitus

Optimistic Bias   Cultural Capital

Typification

Substitution

Habitualisation

Enacted Biography

What You See Is All There Is

Retreating into the Past

"Some of these are worth exploring, so I'll add the following ...

For the Understanding of that which STARTS to STEAM, to the Social Sciences and Humanities Turn – 2

Cognitive Illusions: One important example is that which is grounded in skill, and the illusions that stems from being able to exercise high-level skills at a professional level, but which involve people making judgements that they feel confident to make, but which in fact they are not able to make, but are not aware that they are unable to make – they are ignorant of their ignorance. It is a problem that is reinforced by professional cultures.

Motivated reasoning: A form of reasoning where people access, construct and evaluate arguments in a biased fashion to arrive at or endorse a preferred conclusion. The term *motivated* in motivated reasoning refers to the fact that people use reasoning strategies that allow them to draw the conclusions they want to draw (i.e., are motivated to draw).

For the Understanding of that which STARTS to STEAM, to the Social Sciences and Humanities Turn – 3

Simplism: The unambiguous ascription of single causes and remedies for multi-factored phenomena, providing a clear-cut solution to a clear-cut problem. For example, by having a clear-cut solution in the form of an artist in residence to resolve the clear-cut problem of a creativity deficit.

Retreating into the Past: The past appears attractive, for there one finds things that have been lost, which seemed to work, and which provided answers that people believe worked. Thus do they go backward instead of forward, like the *New Leonardos*, and those who advocate that which now STARTS to STEAM, not understanding that the past matched yesterdays' problems and questions, not those of the future.

For the Understanding of that which STARTS to STEAM, to the Social Sciences and Humanities
Turn – 4

Enacted Biography: A term that refers to a psychological process whereby a biographical pattern, once it becomes known, younger, would-be-artists, begin self-consciously to pattern their lives according to the biographical model. It then becomes constitutive.

Functionalist-reductionist Model of Creativity: A dated view in which creativity is seen as an organisational output (an outcome) to be improved by manipulating independent variables (inputs), for example, by adding an artist to a project team or organisational unit.

Final Logical Interpretant: Habit! This is the habitual attribution of certain significations to certain signs that people are familiar with. Habit is formed by the effect of previous signs.

The Peculiar Case of a Leonardo Lover – 1

The Leonardo Lover is an American creativity (?) consultant. He has it seems (very weirdly?) modelled his life on Leonardo da Vinci (USP?). He has, as consultants do, written a book! It is called How to Think Like Leonardo da Vinci: Seven Steps to Genius Everyday

You might ask if this book is yet another contribution to the (ever growing) mythology surrounding Leonardo. If you are inclined towards critical thinking, you should ask this question!

In his book, the Leonardo Lover criticises increasing specialisation and advocates (yes that word again) the ideal of the Renaissance man or woman – a modern version of – classical liberal arts + some modern perspectives (e.g. computers). It is nevertheless a retreat into the past …

Its also a mythical past, because the book is based on an account of Leonardo's life, written by the Renaissance artist, Giorgio Vasari. Some scholars have presented convincing arguments that the whole work (The Lives of the Most Excellent Painters, Sculptors, and Architects) is a collection of fabrications. Misinformation is indeed everywhere!

The Peculiar Case of a Leonardo Lover – 2

Compare Vasari's account of the death of Leonardo (who is suppose to have died in the arms of the French King!) with Vasari's description of the death of Michelangelo, who died in Rome, and 23 days later, after his body had been returned to Florence, was discovered, when unwrapped (why would you do such a thing in a hot climate?) to not have decomposed at all, and the artist just looked like he was sleeping. Notice something? Both are unrealistic. The key here is to understand that these are neo-platonic accounts of the artists' lives and that biography in those days was not concerned with recounting facts, but with telling a moralising story to inspire people to better things.

The Leonardo Lover just accepts Vasari's Leonardo biography without question, thus ignoring one of the (claimed) attributes of his hero: the questioning of accepted theory and the dogma of his time! The Leonardo Lover STARTS to disprove his own rhetoric!

Worse is to come! the Leonardo Lover claims that: "40 years before Copernicus, da Vinci noted, in large letters for emphasis, 'IL SOLE NO SI MUOVE,' 'The Sun does not move.' He added. 'The earth is not the centre of the circle of the sun, nor in the centre of the universe'."

The Peculiar Case of a Leonardo Lover – 3

Yet, if you read Arthur Koestler's acclaimed account of
man's changing perceptions of the universe – *The
Sleepwalkers* – you will learn that Copernicus did not
conceive the theory of a heliocentric universe and that
he probably learned about it, towards the end of his
Italian studies because it was much discussed in Italy
at the time.

Arthur Koestler also mentions that several other people
also believed in the Heliocentric model, in an earlier
period – medieval times. He names Nicholas of Cusa,
a Cardinal in the Church of Rome no less, as one such
person. So much for the Leonardo Lover's claims in
his book, that in the medieval period all people did
was debate how many angels could fit on the head of
a pin. His book has more of mythology about it, than
historically accurate facts!

It seem that the self-styled *New Leonardo*, is unaware
that the Heliocentric model is discussed in Aristotle's'
work *On the Heavens*, which is probably how people in
the medieval period came to be aware of it, following
the recovery of these works in Europe (translation into
Latin) starting around the mid-12th century.

The Leonardo Lover STARTS indeed to disprove his own
rhetoric ...

Unexpected Item in Bagging Area – STEAM Dazzle: Visual Disruption Intended to Confuse

STEAM Dazzle: Visual Disruption Intended to Confuse (Acrylic and Posca on Canvas Paper)
© Copyright Paul T Kidd 2020

STARTS the Making of Misleading Claims – 1

STARTS now another short story!

According to one of the leading lights in STARTS, Google stole its idea for Street View from an artist. Speaking at a meeting in the City of the Golden Stars, this leading light presented two photos side by side. The one on the left was claimed to be an artist's idea (the Aspen Video Map), the one on the right, a picture of a Google Street View Car.

So where did the artist steal the idea from?

Nazi Street View Perhaps!

Notice the movie camera and cameraman on the
roof of the car in the left foreground

STARTS the Making of Misleading Claims – 2

The idea of mounting a camera on a moving vehicle is an old one, and much used - by the police for example!

Movie Camera in Police Car Puts Evidence on Film

MOUNTED on the dashboard of his patrol car, with its lens pointing forward through the windshield, a motion-picture camera belonging to Officer R. H. Galbraith of the California Highway Patrol takes photographs of the automobiles he trails along the highways, making a permanent film record of any traffic violations for possible later use in court.

There's no arguing with the testimony of this movie camera

STARTS the Making of Misleading Claims – 3

You might be interested to know that the Aspen Video Map was not an artistic project at all, but part of a defence project, funded in the 1970s at MIT using (we presume) 1970s technologies.

Initial work on Google Street View was undertaken by the Stanford University Computer Graphics Lab in a project called The Stanford CityBlock Project: multi-perspective panoramas of city blocks, between 2001 and 2006.

On the Computer Graphics Lab web site you will learn that, what Google eventually implemented is not the exactly the same as what the Computer Graphics Lab implemented.

How similar both are to the systems developed in the 1970s at MIT is anyone's guess. Try making something up for yourself as that seems to be how the STARTS game works.

Perhaps the mythology is more interesting, including the additional feature that the Aspen Video Map idea was stolen from Nazi Street View!

STARTS the Making of Misleading Claims – 4

As we pointed out, earlier, *STARTS* is a socially
constructed reality that operates at the level of
mythology – now you can see what we mean.

Misinformation is everywhere, especially in organisations
that speak with the voice of authority, i.e. the
European Commission.

Let us look at it another way: the European Commission,
specifically its Directorate General called DG
CONNECT, is spending millions of euros – EU tax
payers money – on research that is grounded in
mythology!

Perhaps a better name for DG CONNECT would be DG
DISCONNECTED – from reality!

Strangely this is not, the first time that Europeans have
funded research grounded in mythology.

The last known major example of this occurred in
Germany starting in about 1935. Yes we have to go
back to those nasty Nazis one more time.

STARTS a Consideration of The Ahnenerbe

The Ahnenerbe was a research (?) institute founded by Himmler, essentially researching (?) the origins of the (mythical) Aryan race, and demonstrating that Germans were descended from this (mythical) Aryan race, an advanced (mythical) people from which all other (real) civilisations developed.

It was an exercise in rewriting history to justify Nazi rule of – the whole planet!

It also gave rise to an idea for a series of movies in the 1980s called Indiana Jones and ... The Raiders of the Lost Ark ... and The Last Crusade. Entirely fictional of course, but the Nazi (so-called) archaeology depicted in the films is based on fact, – The Ahnenerbe.

STARTS is the European Commission's very own Ahnenerbe, busy rewriting history and creating its own mythology. For what reasons we wonder? Perhaps we may discover later.

STARTS the Making of Misleading Claims – 5

Perhaps you can now understand why you should not believe anything at all about what emerges from STARTS.

If you do, for reasons of consistency that we mentioned before, next time you are ill, people will expect you to arrange for some blood letting – obviously it makes sense!

And what about STEAM? Yes, more anecdotes, as we will in due course show when we finally start to take apart *The Integration Report*. Anecdotes and more – we promise. Then you will also have some more insights into the Research Integrity Crisis, and the truth behind the statement that all stakeholders are contributing to it: research funding agencies, researchers, their institutions, and publishers. And, we add, bodies that produce reports ...

STARTS a Poem?

STARTS weaving the art-science tangled web,

STARTS new Leonardos in ignorance dwelling,

STARTS the new Medici's power rising,

STARTS the unravelling.

The Research Integrity Crisis – 1

In 2017, in the UK Parliament, the House of Commons Select Committee on Science and Technology started an enquiry in the matter of Research Integrity – actually the lack of Research Integrity.

This was in response to a note (Integrity in Research, POSTNOTE 544) produced by the Parliamentary Office for Science and Technology on the subject of – the growing problem of Research Integrity. Unlike the European Commission's arbitrary approach to ... just about everything it does, this Parliamentary note is based on evidence.

The Research Integrity Crisis – 2

Particularly, the evidence that is now accumulating that shows an increase in the number of retractions of published research papers and cases that are coming to light of practices in academia, research institutes, and industry that are undermining the credibility of scientific research (not just the hard sciences, but also the social sciences as well).

And we add here – the arts and humanities.

At the heart of the problem is not just traditional falsification and fabrication, although that does happen, but what the Americans have come to call Detrimental Research Practices. And the reasons for this are complicated.

The Research Integrity Crisis – 3

In 2017, the National Academy of Sciences in the US
published a report of a study into Research Integrity.
In this report, they define a whole range of activities
that they called Detrimental Research Practices.

Detrimental Research Practices are activities that fall
short of classical scientific fraud – falsification and
fabrication. They include: data manipulations, statistical
manipulations, misuse of databases to produce the
results that people want to produce, misuse of statistics,
unethical publication practices …

The literature quoted in this report expands upon the
practices in more detail. This literature notes many
important issues: the lack of reproducibility when
researchers seek to validate published findings; the
disappearance of negative research results (the growth
of a positive research results bias); people undertaking
research where there is no effect worth investigating,
misuse of statistics especially p-values, small and
unrepresentative sample sizes, researcher incompetence,
etc.

The Research Integrity Crisis — 4

The reasons for the Research Integrity Crisis: pressures
arising from funding shortfalls, pressure to publish
papers, incompetence, lack of professionalism, under
taking research for its publicity value in the news
media, researcher bias, inappropriate research designs
...

That which STARTS to STEAM, is done in an
environment of growing concern about the
disappearance of research integrity.

When looked at in the light of the Research Integrity
Crisis, anyone taking seriously that which STARTS to
STEAM, is likely to find themselves advocating myths
and invented or biased research findings.

That is not to say that, within that which STARTS to
STEAM, there may be no golden threads — it's just
that you are very unlikely ever to find them because
the research record will be thoroughly corrupted,
which was one of the consequences of the Ahnenerbe.

The Research Integrity Crisis – 5

According to the National Academy of Sciences Research Integrity report, with an increasing number of research projects being undertaken by larger groups that bring together a greater diversity of expertise, encompassing a broader range of disciplines striving for a greater degree of synthesis, so the potential for misunderstandings grows. Coordination of research inevitably becomes more complex, and the members of a team may have less familiarity with the discipline-specific practices of other team members, making it more difficult for each collaborator to check and verify the work done by others.

What they are saying is that, in x-disciplinary contexts, you are reliant on other people and need to trust what they say. Evidently that is now a questionable practice. We refer you to the earlier quotes – warnings from the art world and warnings from the social science world.

So are you too, trusting in what that artist is telling you? Or that researcher that is actually operating outside their area of competence, but you (and perhaps the researcher) do not know they are so doing?

The Research Integrity Crisis – 6

Now a quote from the report produced by the House of Commons' Select Committee on Science and Technology, on the matter of Research Integrity:

"The current lack of consistent transparency means that it is impossible to assess the scale of the research integrity issue, leading to accusations that parts of the sector are policing themselves in a secretive way in order to maintain its reputation or, worse, a perception that investigations are not conducted properly in order to avoid embarrassment. Meanwhile, there is a risk that a future high-profile scandal could expose any weaknesses in this arrangement. Fraud appears to be rare, but the number of institutions reporting no investigations each year does not tally with other available information — the self-reported pressures on researchers to compromise on standards, an increase in the rate of journal articles being retracted, and a growth in image manipulation in articles."

Reading the report it seems that those called to give evidence are in denial about the scale of the crisis. Just like people were once in denial about all those claims, concerning abuse of children, directed at people and organisations who spoke with authority, i.e. of high standing in society.

Unexpected Item in Bagging Area – Measure for Measure

Act 3, Scene 2: The street before the prison. Duke Vincentio is speaking at the very end. He starts by saying:

"He who the sword of heaven will bear … "

Vincentio continues his monologue, directed at you, for no-one else is there, until he says:

"O, what may man within him hide, though angel on the outward side!"

Below is a Japanese maple leaf!

Art-science Fakes

Time now to introduce a new concept – art-science fakes.

*An art-science fake is any mythology, false truth claim,
fabrication, falsification, or that which results from
Detrimental Research Practices that relates to the
art-science lovers' symbolic universe, which manifests
in the socially constructed realities of that which
STARTS to STEAM.*

*The art-science lovers' symbolic universe also includes the
art-technology symbolic universe, with the former most
often actually being the latter.*

*That which STARTS to STEAM is full of art-science
fakes – we have already encountered some – more
will follow, especially when we examine the National
Academy of Sciences' document that we called The
Integration Report.*

*As we said – never has it been more important to
question what people and organisations who speak with
authority are saying. The Integration Report is a clear
demonstration of this need.*

What Relevance a 500 years dead Aristotelian?

Leonardo da Vinci – the real one not the mythical one –
is here and wishes to speak:

"Indeed I do. I want to present my latest scientific results
for, I [...] proved that the part of the moon which
shines consists of water [...] and that the reason the
waters of the moon [...] do not descend to the centre
of the universe and to join itself to the earth, [...] is
clear sign that the moon is clothed with her own
elements, namely water, air and fire [...]". *

So now you have met the real Leonardo, not the mythical
one, the mythology of whom must qualify as the
greatest art-science fake of all!

*Extracted from the Note Books of Leonardo da Vinci

Defining Knowledge

And now it is time to define knowledge!

The Philosopher's definition: Knowledge is justified true belief.

The sociologist's definition: Knowledge is that which a sufficient number of people believe to be true (which thereby excludes individual idiosyncratic beliefs).

The case of Leonardo illustrates. Much of what is known about Leonardo is knowledge in the sociological sense, but not the philosophical sense. The Leonardo story is mostly myth, tall tales, fabrication, falsification, exaggeration, misunderstanding, false beliefs, interpretation, wishful thinking, fantasy, etc.. mixed up with a little knowledge in the philosophical sense. This demonstrates that reality is socially constructed – there are no exceptions. Even those dedicated to seeking objective truth, are caught-up in socially constructed realities. Put another way, their minds are full of knowledge in the sociological sense! You can check by asking them if they believe the Leonardo story!

Defining Knowledge

These two definitions of knowledge are very useful. What you will find in The Integration Report is mostly knowledge in the sociological sense mixed up with some knowledge in the philosophical sense.

In essence the experts who wrote the report were seeking to socially construct reality (in a form that is convenient to them)!

Did they succeed? Put another way – did you believe?

Another question: do you prefer their reality and thus, will you ignore the little boy who is telling you that the Emperor is wearing no clothes?

If you do prefer The Integration Report's socially constructed reality, you could end-up doing tremendous damage to the education of STEM people, with long term damaging consequences for your country and its people.

What will it be then?

How do you Slow Down the Progress of Science?

In a 1948 short story, *The Mark Gable Foundation*, Mark Gable believes that scientific progress is too fast and wants to know how to slow it down. In response he is told that he should "[...] set up a Foundation, with an annual endowment of thirty million dollars. Research workers in need of funds could apply for grants, if they could make out a convincing case. Have ten committees, each composed of twelve scientists, appointed to pass on these applications. Take the most active scientists out of the laboratory and make them members of these committees. And the very best men in the field should be appointed as Chairmen at salaries of $50,000 each. Also have about twenty prizes of $100,000 each for the best scientific papers of the year. This is just about all you would have to do."

How do you Slow Down the Progress of Science?

Gable is then told why this would be effective in slowing down the progress of science: "First of all, the best scientists would be removed from their laboratories and kept busy on committees passing on applications for funds. Secondly, the scientific workers in need of funds will concentrate on problems which are considered promising and are pretty certain to lead to publishable results. For a few years there may be a great increase in scientific output; but by going after the obvious, pretty soon Science will dry out. Science will become something like a parlour game. Some things will be considered interesting, others will not. There will be fashions. Those who follow the fashion will get grants. Those who won't, will not, and pretty soon they will learn to follow the fashion too."

There is now an easier way: join the grazing herd of the art-science lovers, get yourself an artist-in-residence, and take up Mode 3 Knowledge Production ...

93

Mode 3 Knowledge Production – 1

Time now to introduce another new concept, – Mode 3 Knowledge Production.

To fully understand this point, you will need to be familiar with Mode 1 and Mode 2 Knowledge Production as defined in the 1994 book with the title The New Production of Knowledge: The Dynamics of Science and Research in Contemporary Societies by Michael Gibbons and five colleagues.

A follow-up to the above is the 2001 book with the title Re-Thinking Science: Knowledge and the Public in an Age of Uncertainty by three of the authors of the 1994 book.

I know – reading books! Not to worry though, for it is not required in Mode 3 Knowledge Production!

Mode 3 Knowledge Production – 2

Mode 3 Knowledge Production is developing along side *Mode 1* and *Mode 2 Knowledge Production*, and may replace both if something drastic is not done to stop this. *Mode 3 Knowledge Production* takes place within a specific context – the context of technocracy, ignorance, incompetence, corrupt relationships, unaccountable power, lack of morality, and the availability of enormous public resources. This context defines the totality of the environment in which both problems and their solutions are fabricated.

Mode 3 Knowledge Production is ill disciplined – ill-disciplinary. Standard, due diligence procedures, such as defining and understanding the state-of-the-art, are completely discarded in favour of an approach that is best described as *whatever people believe is true will do*.

Another characteristic of *Mode 3 Knowledge Production* is the diversity of stakeholders involved – in fact anyone can undertake *Mode 3 Knowledge Production* as it requires no research skills and competencies at all.

Mode 3 Knowledge Production – 3

A fourth characteristic of *Mode 3 Knowledge Production* is that it requires people to constantly refer to critical thinking, while rigorously avoiding any critical thinking, because reflexivity is most definitely not needed.

A novel feature of *Mode 3 Knowledge Production* is that no quality control is required, as the aim is to adopt approaches that, in *Mode 1 and 2 Knowledge Production* are referred to as *Fabrication and Falsification*, as well as *Detrimental Research Practices*. This is done to maximise the transfer of public resources into the hands of *Mode 3 Knowledge Production* participants, because *Mode 3 Knowledge Production* conveniently always produces the results that you want, which is the hallmark of its success.

Mode 3 Knowledge Production – 4

A very special feature of *Mode 3 Knowledge Production* is that, it entirely operates at the level of mythology, seeking to rewrite history and establish ideology as fact, thus ensuring continuity of funding for *Mode 3 Knowledge Production* participants.

An added benefit is that, it is also very easy for *Mode 3 Knowledge Production* participants to rebuff any form of criticism, as all they have to say is that the person doing the criticising, 'doesn't understand', and for some mysterious reason, many people accept this! No critical thinking needed!

Traces of *Mode 3 Knowledge Production* can be found across the globe, but the European Union is a pioneer and a world-leader in this field. The pioneering steps were taken in early days of the German National Socialist European Union, in 1935, under an initiative called the Ahnenerbe. These ground-breaking advances are being continued today, in the latest European Union, in an initiative called STARTS. *Mode 3 Knowledge Production* – you know it makes sense!

How to Prosper in a Mode 3 Knowledge Production Environment

"Hype your work, slice the findings up as much as possible (four papers good, two papers bad), compress the results (most top journals have little space, a typical *Nature* letter now has the density of a black hole), simplify your conclusions but complexify the material (more difficult for reviewers to fault it!), mine rich sources of data, even if they lack originality. Most damagingly, it has become profitable to ignore or hide results that do not fit with the story being sold – a mix of evidence tends to make a paper look messy and lower its appeal."

Peter A. Lawrence (Cambridge University) 2007

The Integration Report: Sir Eric Ashby Speaks from 1958

Preparing for our full encounter with *The Integration Report*, Sir Eric Ashby, FRS, speaks from the past:

"The antithesis between science and humanism has almost vanished, but it has been replaced by another antithesis, equally mischievous. The future historian will record that the unprofitable debates of the 1860s on the humanities versus science were followed in the 1950s by equally unprofitable debates on specialisation versus a liberal education."

The future historian may also say of the early part of the 21st century, that both antitheses were rekindled again in clouds of STEAM!

The Integration Report: Sir Eric Ashby Speaks from 1958

Preparing for our full encounter with The Integration Report, Sir Eric Ashby, FRS, speaks for a second time from the past:

"Much of the confusion of ideas which attended the first debate reappears in the second. Specialisation, for example, is commonly identified with science and technology, and a liberal education is identified with arts subjects. It has been forgotten that liberality is a spirit of pursuit, not a choice of subject; and no account is taken of the fact that a boy who goes up on the classical side at school and then takes 'Greats' at Oxford has had the most specialised education in Europe and is likely to be innocent of the most elementary knowledge of subjects on which Newton, Faraday, Darwin, and Rutherford spent their lives; whereas by contrast even the meanest engineering graduate has spent eight years or so on history, English, French; he has an inkling of what Shakespeare wrote; he has some rudimentary appreciation of what Abraham Lincoln did for humanity."

The Integration Report: Sir Eric Ashby Speaks from 1958

Preparing for our full encounter with The Integration Report, Sir Eric Ashby, FRS, speaks for a third time from the past:

"What then is missing in a scientific or technological education? It is not a smattering of art or architecture which is missing, nor is it an acquaintance with history or literature. Indeed it is not a primary lack of subject-matter at all: the fault lies with what Alfred Whitehead called a celibacy of the intellect, which is divorced from the concrete contemplation of the complete facts. It is a preoccupation with abstractions from reality, an escape from the whole of reality. In his book, Science and the Modern World, Whitehead warned us that this would become the great danger of professional education. Each profession, he said, makes progress in its own groove of abstractions, but there is no groove of abstractions which is adequate for the comprehension of human life."

*The Integration Report: Sir Eric Ashby Speaks
from 1958*

*Preparing for our full encounter with The Integration
Report, Sir Eric Ashby, FRS, speaks for a fourth time
from the past:*

*"Adaptations needed to bring British universities into
equilibrium with the age of technology are changes of
curriculum; they could be accomplished through the
normal channels of university administration and
legislation. But they would not be successful unless
accompanied by subtle adaptations in academic
thought: professors of technology need to be persuaded
that the pattern of curriculum under which they
themselves were trained is inadequate for their
students. Professors of arts subjects need to be
persuaded that the presence of technology in
universities puts them under an obligation to
reconsider the emphasis in their own humanistic
studies ...*

The Integration Report: Sir Eric Ashby Speaks from 1958

Preparing for our full encounter with *The Integration Report*, Sir Eric Ashby, FRS, speaks for a fifth time from the past:

"It is at this point that universities look to their faculties of arts for help; and it is at this point that they are often disappointed. For faculties of arts have themselves become so deeply influenced by science that they seem unable to offer help towards the assimilation of technologists. Instead of contributing to the university what the Victorians understood by a liberal education, some of them are doing with grammar and documents what scientists and technologists can already do with formulae and instruments. This is doubtless profitable for the progress of scholarship in the humanities, but one cannot escape the consequences that humanities cease to be humanising when they are treated that way. It is a sort of treatment which leads to a celibacy of the intellect, as inimical to a liberal education in arts as it is in science."

Unexpected Item in Bagging Area – Blake's Proverbs of Hell

From William Blake's *The Marriage of Heaven and Hell*:

In seed time learn, in harvest teach, in winter enjoy.

Drive your cart and your plough over the bones of the dead.

The road of excess leads to the palace of wisdom.

Prudence is a rich ugly old maid courted by Incapacity.

He who desires but acts not, breeds pestilence.

The cut worm forgives the plough.

Dip him in the river who loves water.

A fool sees not the same tree that a wise man sees.

He whose face gives no light, shall never become a star.

Eternity is in love with the productions of time.

The busy bee has no time for sorrow.

The hours of folly are measured by the clock, but of wisdom: no clock can measure.

All wholesome food is caught without a net or a trap.

Bring out number weight & measure in a year of dearth.

No bird soars too high, if he soars with his own wings.

A dead body, revenges not injuries.

The most sublime act is to set another before you.

If the fool would persist in his folly he would become wise.

Folly is the cloak of knavery.

Shame is Prides cloak.

Our Fictitious Future Historian Speaks

In Response to *The Integration Report* and Sir Eric Ashby's observations from the past, our fictitious future historian says:

"Young people of the early 21st century, had already received a liberal arts education – a modern version of – by the time they attended university. This modern liberal arts education included all the subjects listed by Ashby (and more).

"Why, given that Alfred Whitehead had so clearly articulated the issues in 1927, were people, 90 years later, still having to do so?

"Why was it that, in the early 21st century, few if any, including those with liberal arts educations, or who were proclaiming themselves to be New Leonardos, had noticed what Ashby wrote in 1958? Or indeed what Whitehead wrote in 1927?"

Siren Voices Among all that Cloudy STEAM

"In an essay written for the *Scientific American's* blog in 2012, Steven Ross Pomeroy notes that the concept of bringing together arts and science is not a new one. In fact, our efforts to create this convergence within the twenty-first century hark back to much earlier times: Leonardo da Vinci brought the two together in Renaissance Italy. It appears that, even within contemporary times, those at the forefront of innovation have been merging arts and science practice. Pomeroy notes that *"Nobel laureates in the sciences are seventeen times likelier than the average scientist to be a painter, twelve times as likely to be a poet, and four times as likely to be a musician"*.

These words are taken from another artists' advocacy report called *A New STEAM Age: Challenging the STEM Agenda in Research*.

See – they want a share of all that STEM funding!

Notice the art-science fakes. Two actually. One we have already encountered, the other, is yet to appear – *Art Fosters Scientific Success*: anecdotes, myths, and some highly questionable research. We are back to the matter of the Research Integrity Crisis.

Two Issues Disentangled

Time to disentangle two issues:

Issue 1: What some people call the culture sector, in which we include art galleries, theatre and entertainment, the games industry, film, TV, music, fashion, arts and crafts, and such forth, is a sector that has experienced significant growth and has become very important economically. You will definitely encounter people with artistic backgrounds in this sector often working as designers, curators, directors, content creators, artisans, etc.

Issue 2: Art and artists foster scientific success, innovation, and creativity, and artists can generally work magic and solve all problems, including improving all the deficits and shortcomings that apparently exist in the formal education of STEM professionals. And the great myth that art drives science and technology … Ka-Ching!

In this work we are addressing Issue 2.

How Insulting Can You Be?

Those advocating that which STARTS to STEAM often resort to insulting STEM people to justify their arguments:

European Commission, DG DISCONNECTED meeting: "Engineers struggle with creativity."

European Commission, DG DISCONNECTED Call for Proposals: "The challenge is to accelerate and widen the exchange of skills of artists and creative people with entrepreneurs and technologists ... "

An IMechE Article: "Adding art to engineering education teaches the kind of risk-taking approach and creative problem solving that can be applied to the world's biggest problems ... "

The formulae is always very similar: create a duality of creatives (artists) vs. non-creatives (STEM people) (often while criticising the art vs. STEM duality!) and in doing so insinuate that STEM people have a creativity deficit, which can be resolved by adding an artist to your team, group, project, company ... Ka-Ching!

How Insulting Can You Be?

People who do this, do so because they have no other way of justifying their case – thus do they insult the very people they are seeking to supply them with funds. Strange behaviour!

Last time I looked I did not notice any shortage of creativity among STEM people.

Those who adopt this somewhat counter-productive approach are demonstrating that they have a very dated belief. There is a name for this belief. It is called the Functionalist-Reductive Model of creativity.

In honour of such people, we have created a special product – we call it Artist's Creativity Elixir. This was specially formulated for the European Commission's DG DISCONNECTED to solve what they perceive as the European Union's creativity deficit.

As the UK is not a member of the European Union, we do not suffer anymore from this deficit – we cured ourselves by leaving the European Union and you can see why we did so!

Artist's Creativity Elixir – 1

Artist's Creativity Elixir – 2

Artist's Creativity Elixir has some very special properties:

It is highly toxic and should be used with great caution. It is very easy to overdose. Those who do so might find themselves questioning DG DISCONNECTED and the European Commission and its unaccountable power. Indeed they might see through the smoke and mirrors that hides the true nature of the European Union from its citizens, and might even take to exercising their sovereign right to political self-determination and seek to overthrow and destroy the insult to Parliamentary Democracy that is the European Union.

It has the special property that it is invisible. Thus anyone who tells you that the bottles are empty, is not telling you the truth. We have noted that those who hold to the Functionalist-Reductive Model and many others too, have a prior inclination to say that the bottles are empty.

In Case You do not Know ...

Note the difference in meaning:

- *Hobby: An activity done regularly in one's leisure time for pleasure.*

- *Avocation: a subordinate occupation pursued in addition to one's vocation especially for enjoyment.*

An avocation can be a hobby, but it is one pursued as a minor occupation. The implication is that it is more consuming than just a hobby. The root of each word is different. Hobby comes from Late Middle English hobyn, hoby, pet names for a robin. Later it came to denote a toy horse or hobby horse, hence an activity done for pleasure. Avocation is Mid 17th century: from Latin avocatio(n-), from avocare 'call away', from ab- 'from' + vocare 'to call'.

It may seem to be a matter of semantics, but the difference is important, as you will discover soon. Why say avocation, when you could just say hobby? Or perhaps we should ask: why say hobby when you can say avocation? The answer has to do with the mythology of the art-science lovers' symbolic universe.

How to Spot an Art-Science Lover

Art-science lovers are fairly easy to spot, once you have the knowledge. Here is a quick guide:

Art-science lovers unquestionably accept anything they are told that fits with their ideology. Generally they do not display any critical thinking towards that which reinforces their beliefs. They have a tendency to rewrite history to make it fit with their ideology. They can be found claiming that art and science were once one, or that art and science are very similar. They might also claim that companies are stealing ideas from artists. They might too say, that people filling patents and establishing new companies as a result, are artistically trained. They may also regale you with anecdotal tales from a distant past, when life was simpler and much less was known, when the science and engineering professions were not yet formed (or were still in the early stages of formation), when division of labour was very different than it is today, when gentleman and well-off people did some art, while also doing a bit of science or engineering. Generally they also have a wish to time travel – to the distant past that they romanticise about. Some may even use p-values ...

113

Self-serving Platitudes – 1

Self-serving platitudes: Graduates in the 21st century, need to be good communicators, critical thinkers, team workers, creative problem solvers, lifelong learners.

Statements like this appear many times in The Integration Report (and elsewhere too). They appear over, and over and over again … Repetitively so!

There is nothing 21st century about these skills! They have been relevant since the 19th century, but became increasingly so as the 20th century progressed. Any idea why? You won't find the answer in The Integration Report, nor among that which STARTS to STEAM.

They are also mostly these days, skills that children learn at school. Let us not here insult the teaching profession by claiming that this is not so.

Self-serving Platitudes – 2

Self-serving platitudes: Integration of knowledge is necessary to address the challenges of our time.

Statements like this appear in The Integration Report (and elsewhere too). In several places in fact, in slightly different forms. It is after all, an integration report – which is, it transpires, confused about integration!

If you care to look, most challenges in the real world require knowledge from many different disciplines and sources to be brought together. This has been so for a very long time. It is not a new requirement. How to do this is important, but it is context specific, involves factors beyond the reach of education, and, some people/organisations do it well, others less so.

Notice we did not say that "knowledge needs to be integrated". That is because integration of knowledge means what exactly? Evidently, given the vagueness that surrounds the word integration, the authors of The Integration Report do not know what integration of knowledge means either!

A Life Spent Solving Problems!

Problem solving is much mentioned in *The Integration Report*. In several places in fact, in slightly different forms.

A life spent in *STEM* seems to be a life spent solving problems – complex or otherwise.

Here is a list of simple *STEM* related problems: Oh dear! We could not think of any!

Here is a list of complex problems: all problems are complex in various ways and in varying degrees! That is why we resort to simplifications and then take steps to deal with the consequences of this.

Here is a list of work that engineers do, that does not necessarily involve solving problems: investigations; evaluations and assessments; testing and commissioning; participation in management; advising; monitoring; organising; improving; ...

Unexpected Item in Bagging Area – Blake's Proverbs of Hell

From William Blake's *The Marriage of Heaven and Hell*:

Prisons are built with stones of Law, Brothels with bricks of Religion.

The pride of the peacock is the glory of God.

The lust of the goat is the bounty of God.

The wrath of the lion is the wisdom of God.

The nakedness of woman is the work of God.

Excess of sorrow laughs. Excess of joy weeps.

The roaring of lions, the howling of wolves, the raging of the stormy sea, and the destructive sword, are portions of eternity too great for the eye of man.

The fox condemns the trap, not himself.

Joys impregnate. Sorrows bring forth.

Let man wear the fell of the lion, woman the fleece of the sheep.

The bird a nest, the spider a web, man friendship.

The selfish smiling fool, & the sullen frowning fool, shall be both thought wise, that they may be a rod.

What is now proved was once only imagined.

The rat, the mouse, the fox, the rabbit: watch the roots; the lion, the tiger, the horse, the elephant, watch the fruits.

The cistern contains; the fountain overflows.

One thought, fills immensity.

Always be ready to speak your mind, and a base man will avoid you.

Every thing possible to be believed is an image of truth.

The Enlightening Case of Dorothy Johansen – 1

*It is 1949, and before an audience in Portland, Oregan,
Dr Johansen, an associate professor of history, is
speaking about The Integrative Method of Teaching.*

*She is referring to integration in its pedagogical aspect:
the method of relating varieties of subject matter to
units of study or to problem solving situations.*

*"Several methods have been advanced," she says, "by
which integration might be achieved, and all are
called integrative."*

She then names one of these: Correlation.

*Correlation has as its objective a broader comprehension
of one field of study or subject by associating it with
another.*

*She then gives an example from her personal
experience ...*

The Enlightening Case of Dorothy Johansen – 2

She refers back to the 1930s, and two courses: one in literature covering the period from Homeric Greece to the mid 18th century, and another in history covering the same period.

Students were required to take both courses during their first year. These courses both covered the same period at approximately the same pace, and it was believed that the students would get a complete and unified picture of past civilisations.

Each course referred to materials of the other, but emphasised the particular technics of that discipline – literature emphasised content, composition and criticism; history emphasised content, historical approach and method.

The integrative factor, was the student who, it was hoped, would draw from these two approaches and two bodies of subject matter a picture of the whole civilisation they presented.

The Enlightening Case of Dorothy Johansen – 3

"The correlation," she says, "has the advantages not
found in the isolated treatment of either of the
subjects."

But it was not considered to be sufficiently integrated
for the purpose of general education as she and her
colleagues conceived it. So in 1939 they merged the
two courses into one and called it Humanities.

The new course addressed a whole picture of a temporal
and spatial phenomenon called western civilisation. It
covered literature, art forms, philosophy, science,
politics and economy of the various peoples who made
up that civilisation.

The introduction was not superficial, nor a finished
portrait. The student was required to get a personal
and more penetrating understanding through reading
first hand records of the era they were studying.

The course provided common lectures, but students also
worked in small groups to discuss significant
problems that emerge from the data being examined.

The Enlightening Case of Dorothy Johansen — 4

She tells her audience that, "we believe that we have
   not sacrificed the basic principles of the
   disciplines that have been fused. Rather we have
   given the students the elementary tools for later
   specialised work in literature, history and the
   social sciences."

The course as structured, and the teaching, she
   believes, are no more than a device which helps
   students to function on their own in an
   integrative process.

But then she states "not all subject matter can be
   easily integrated with other subject matter, and
   peripheral material which is pertinent may be
   sacrificed or subject matter may be forced into an
   unnatural unity."

Thus Dr Johansen issues this caveat: "Integration of
   courses can be successfully accomplished only
   where a common approach is possible, and where
   there is a related body of material exemplifying a
   significant, meaningful whole."

The Enlightening Case of Dorothy Johansen – 5

She then points to a further difficulty – the one of
meeting requirements for more advanced specialised
work when courses have been fused. She points to
two different arguments in this respect.

Argument 1: Elementary courses should be limited to
providing special preparation for further and more
difficult training. If elementary training is to be
properly done, then there is no time to bring in
anything else.

Argument 2: The best possible preparation for a
specialised course is derived from an integrated
approach through relevant subjects, since a broad
background gives the fundamental understanding
which in turn gives greater meaning to the special
technics developed in the advanced course.

She then however highlights another difficulty related
to the student: "over enthusiasm has led some to
consider integrating technics as the solution to all
educational problems, which it is not."

The Enlightening Case of Dorothy Johansen – 6

On this matter of the student and the over-enthusiasm for integration she further says: "On the level of primary and secondary education it is probably true that integration facilitates learning and gives it greater meaning for all types of students. But I am afraid that this is not true for all college students regardless of their ability."

In particular she highlights that there is a group of students for whom integration is not going to work: those that do not have the ability to abstract, which is something that is needed in integrative learning.

We leave you with this observation from Dr Johansen: "Although some of us are reluctant to concede the fact, our colleges and professions are now demanding broader areas of academic experience for their graduates, and this movement indicates that the era of extreme specialization is over. Somewhere between the extremists' views lies the happy compromise which would provide a well-rounded background for professional competence and personal growth."

Time to leave 1949 behind and return to 2020, a journey of 71 years ...

The Enlightening Case of Dorothy Johansen – 7

And after time travelling for 71 years we arrive back in 2020 and then ask this question: to what extent are STEM courses already integrated in the pedagogical sense just explored? And in other ways?

We also ask: is there more to a STEM course than just a collection of STEM subjects?

We then ask: is there, anywhere in The Integration Report, any consideration of the issues raised 71 years ago by Dorothy Johansen?

We also ask: is there, anywhere in The Integration Report, any consideration of the inter-relationship among subjects that come together to form a STEM course?

We leave you to ponder these questions …

For the Understanding of that which STARTS to STEAM, to the Statisticians Turn – 1

We previously mentioned *p-values* for a reason!

Statistical significance is in trouble, specifically the (mis)use of *p-values*, and also confidence intervals.

Statisticians have correlated False Discovery Rates (False Positives) with *p-values* using different approaches: Bayesian and Frequentist approaches as well as conditional probabilities.

The results are alarming: with a *p-value* of 0.05 the False Positive rate is at least 23%, but could typically be 50%. It depends ... But the point is that *p-values* are misleading, and the situation gets worse when bias creeps in or is deliberately introduced. Or when the research has been incompetently done!

For the Understanding of that which STARTS to STEAM, to the Statisticians Turn – 2

Some journals have banned the use of p-values in papers!

The mis-use of p-values in connection with the reproducibility crisis (part of the Research Integrity Crisis), has highlighted that there have been concerns expressed for decades about misunderstandings and mis-interpretations of the meaning of p-values.

In 2016, the American Statistical Association took the unusual step of issuing a statement on Statistical Significance and P-Values ...

For the Understanding of that which STARTS to STEAM, to the Statisticians Turn – 3

The American Statistical Association 2016 statement on Statistical Significance and P-Values: Principles

- *P-values can indicate how incompatible the data are with a specified statistical model.*

- *P-values do not measure the probability that the studied hypothesis is true, or the probability that the data were produced by chance alone.*

- *Scientific conclusions and business or policy decisions should not be based only on whether a p-value passes a specific threshold.*

- *Proper inference requires full reporting and transparency.*

- *A p-value, or statistical significance, does not measure the size of an effect or the importance of a result.*

- *By itself, a p-value does not provide a good measure of evidence regarding a model or hypothesis.*

For the Understanding of that which STARTS to STEAM, to the Statisticians Turn – 4

Statisticians are now stressing the importance of replication studies, of effect sizes, of the plausibility of alternative hypotheses, of proper experimental design, of avoiding under-powered studies, and of using subject area knowledge to interpret results.

In the paper that contains the American Statistical Association 2016 statement on the principles of Statistical Significance and P-Values, they say:

— *"Of special note is the following article, which is a significant contribution to the literature about p-values and statistical significance: Greenland, S., Senn, S.J., Rothman, K.J., Carlin, J.B., Poole, C., Goodman, S.N. and Altman, D.G.: "Statistical Tests, P-values, Confidence Intervals, and Power: A Guide to Misinterpretations."*

For the Understanding of that which STARTS to STEAM, to the Statisticians Turn – 5

This paper lists many common misinterpretations of p-values, p-value comparisons and predictions, confidence intervals, and power. One in particular we here note concerning the following fallacy, that: 'the p-value for the null hypothesis is the probability that chance alone produced the observed association'.

This is a common fallacy. To say that chance alone produced the observed association is logically equivalent to asserting that every assumption used to compute the p-value is correct, including the null hypothesis. Thus to claim that the null p-value is the probability that chance alone produced the observed association is completely backwards: the p-value is a probability computed assuming chance was operating alone. The absurdity of the common backwards interpretation might be appreciated by pondering how the p-value, which is a probability deduced from a set of assumptions (the statistical model), can possibly refer to the probability of those assumptions."

Which leads us to these observations ...

For the Understanding of that which STARTS to STEAM, to the Statisticians Turn – 6

Quoting from Greenland, et al:

"Careful interpretation also demands critical examination of the assumptions and conventions used for the statistical analysis—not just the usual statistical assumptions, but also the hidden assumptions about how results were generated and chosen for presentation."

"Significance tests and confidence intervals do not by themselves provide a logically sound basis for concluding an effect is present or absent with certainty or a given probability. This point should be borne in mind whenever one sees a conclusion framed as a statement of probability, likelihood, or certainty about a hypothesis. Information about the hypothesis beyond that contained in the analyzed data and in conventional statistical models (which give only data probabilities) must be used to reach such a conclusion; that information should be explicitly acknowledged and described by those offering the conclusion."

For the Understanding of that which STARTS to STEAM, to the Statisticians Turn – 7

Quoting from Greenland, et al:

"All statistical methods (whether frequentist or Bayesian, or for testing or estimation, or for inference or decision) make extensive assumptions about the sequence of events that led to the results presented—not only in the data generation, but in the analysis choices. Thus, to allow critical evaluation, research reports (including meta-analyses) should describe in detail the full sequence of events that led to the statistics presented, including the motivation for the study, its design, the original analysis plan, the criteria used to include and exclude subjects (or studies) and data, and a thorough description of all the analyses that were conducted."

Unexpected Item in Bagging Area – Blake's Proverbs of Hell

From William Blake's *The Marriage of Heaven and Hell*:

The fox provides for himself, but God provides for the lion.

Think in the morning. Act in the noon. Eat in the evening. Sleep in the night.

He who has suffered you to impose on him knows you.

As the plough follows words, so God rewards prayers.

The tigers of wrath are wiser than the horses of instruction.

Expect poison from the standing water.

You never know what is enough unless you know what is more than enough.

Listen to the fools reproach! it is a kingly title!

The eyes of fire, the nostrils of air, the mouth of water, the beard of earth.

The weak in courage is strong in cunning.

The apple tree never asks the beech how he shall grow, nor the lion, the horse, how he shall take his prey.

The thankful receiver bears a plentiful harvest.

If others had not been foolish, we should be so.

The soul of sweet delight, can never be defiled.

When thou sees an Eagle, thou sees a portion of Genius, lift up thy head!

As the caterpillar chooses the fairest leaves to lay her eggs on, so the priest lays his curse on the fairest joys.

To create a little flower is the labour of ages.

Damn, braces: Bless relaxes.

The best wine is the oldest, the best water the newest.

For the Understanding of that which STARTS to STEAM, to the Humanities Turn – 1

If you are a STEM person or a Social Science person, you may wonder if the Humanities fields can add any value in research. We will now show you that they can, by demonstrating what they offer by way of supporting a critical reading of The Integration Report.

We will look into several areas where we will find the concepts that will help to aid your understanding. In fact we will do more than aid your understanding – we will reveal things that you are very unlikely to discover in other ways!

We will focus on that which is concerned with the analysis and interpretation of texts, that can, enable your resistance …

For the Understanding of that which STARTS to STEAM, to the Humanities Turn – 2

We begin with – hermeneutics.

Hermeneutics is not a discipline, but a way of knowing.

Hermeneutics is concerned with the interpretation of texts. What do texts mean?

Traditionally hermeneutics is linked to religion and law. The interpretation of religious texts, the interpretation of legal texts.

Hermeneutics though can be, and is, applied to other types of texts.

An important feature of hermeneutics is context. You cannot understand or interpret texts unless you know something about the context in which they were created.

Thus we need to examine the context of *The Integration Report* and (some of) its content. Actually we have already been doing this!

For the Understanding of that which STARTS to STEAM, to the Humanities Turn – 3

Continuing, we consider – intertextuality.

Intertextuality is a concept. The Oxford Dictionary of Media and Communication, defines intertextuality as: the various links in form and content, which bind any text to other texts.

At a basic level the use of references is an aspect of intertextuality. Genre is also an aspect of intertexuality.

The meanings of texts are derived from the meanings of other texts which they reference, or sometimes do not reference, but are still associated. More context!

The external relations of The Integration Report, with other texts can be investigated. This is very revealing.

Another concept is intratextuality which is the internal relations within a given text, such as the relations between captions and images, which brings us to something very important ...

For the Understanding of that which STARTS to STEAM, to the Humanities Turn – 4

And what is important is – socio-cultural linguistics.

Socio-cultural linguistics is the study of language in a socio-cultural context.

What is of interest is the concept that texts, written and spoken, emerge from combinations of discourses, possibly contradictory, sometimes vague and agentless, other times explicit, containing actors with agency, sometimes authoritarian, other times liberal.

What binds these discourses together is ideology, which brings the different discourses into a particular configuration which are mutually supportive, or which seeks to resolve, in one direction or another, differences among incommensurable discourses.

Also prominent in socio-cultural linguistics is the idea, once again, of context.

Do the Humanities Really Humanise?

We ask this question because Sir Eric Ashby noted that they do not necessarily do so.

There is some truth in the observation that Humanities subjects have become more quantitative, more scientific. Aspects of Linguistics for example.

There is a claim by some in the Humanities, that humanities subjects are needed because they do humanise.

Does that mean that STEM subjects dehumanise?

The problem of dehumanisation – comes from where? From disciplines? Or from society and personality types? Oh dear, we are complicating matters. But this is precisely the issue.

Implying that STEM people are de-humanised by their disciplines is just stereotyping people. Of course you will find people who seem to have been dehumanised, but you will also find people in the arts and humanities who also seem to have been de-humanised.

A Poem

Here is a poem. We wrote it to integrate art into this work, to make you feel more human:

Shades of green from eternity spring,
In mind's glades, beauty never dims.

Feeling more human?

For the Understanding of that which STARTS to STEAM, to the Humanities Turn – 5

And now we are ready to begin ...

To take apart The Integration Report to see what discourses lie therein, and what ideology binds them together.

To establish its context.

To explore its intertextuality.

To scrutinize its content and what it means.

To examine the veracity of its claims.

. . .

The Integration Report – Its Conclusions

The Integration Report says that the available evidence is sufficient to urge support for courses and programs that integrate the arts and humanities with STEMM in higher education.

This is the conclusion that they were always going to reach! Surely you did not expect that they would conclude otherwise? The outcome is predefined by the reason for the study, which was not about integration of arts and humanities into STEMM courses in higher education per-se. This was just a surrogate for the real reason for the study.

In fact, there is no evidence to support the conclusion that arts and humanities should be integrated with STEMM in higher education, because all the study found were a lot of anecdotes from artists and art-science lovers, and a few cases which turn out to be deeply flawed ...

The Integration Report – Its Discourses ...

We want now to mention some of the discourses that are evident in *The Integration Report.* We have noted several. Here are a few obvious ones:

- *The Discourse of Authority*

- *The Pleading the Case Discourse*

- *The Evidence Discourse*

- *The Suffer the Little Children Discourse*

- *The Deficit Discourse*

- *The Integration Discourse*

What do we mean?

The Integration Report – Its Discourses ...

The Discourse of Authority is the report, saying we are the National Academy of Sciences, founded at the behest of Abraham Lincoln no less, independent of government ... trustworthy. And through selected experts – trustworthy experts – we will carefully investigate ... This discourse is presented in the language of a study brief and assurances that, through evidence we will get to the truth, regardless, because that's what the National Academy of Sciences does, which contradicts the next discourse ...

The Pleading the Case Discourse does what it says – pleads the case, based on little evidence, which, even when it seems sound, is not – as we will soon demonstrate. Because of the lack of evidence, supporting *The Pleading the Case Discourse*, and upon which the *Discourse of Authority* relies, a need is created for ...

The Evidence Discourse which tries to save the *Discourse of Authority* by providing an excuse for the lack of sound evidence, by specifically drawing attention to the issue of anecdotes, and trying to justifying anecdotes as an acceptable form of evidence. This glaring weakness helps to explain the appearance of a very strange discourse ...

The Integration Report – Its Discourses ...

The Suffer the Little Children Discourse, addresses the education of very young (Infant) school children through the use of art. Recall the report is supposed to be addressing undergraduate and graduate education! That the Suffer the Little Children Discourse is present seems strange, but is not when one considers the ideology that binds the discourses together, which requires ...

The Deficit Discourse, is a necessity as it raises, in the mind of the reader, the idea that there is some problem that is in need of resolution, some shortfall, and some deficit that can only be resolved through integration, thus ...

The Integration Discourse is central, but is – surprisingly? – often very vague! Integration it seems means many things, but nothing it seems, consistently specific in this report, except that it does have a specific meaning, which stands out from the other meanings – the clue is in the title!

The Integration Report – Its Ideology

What ideology binds these discourses together?

This ideology: a backward looking one, that foregrounds one group of actors – artists – who are the only group in the report who consistently appear, over and over, as active agents, bringing about integration, even though integration is often somewhat vague. And when artists themselves are not agents, then scientists become the agents, by becoming artists ...

There is another National Academies report where the ideology is spelt out clearly.

That report is called *Collaborations of Consequence: NAKFI's 15 Years Igniting Innovation at the Intersections of Disciplines*. In this report you will discover the ideology of *The Integration Report* which is that the Renaissance was an *integrative period* of unified knowledge—a time during which art and science were one [recall how to spot an art-science lover!]. *Homo Universalis*, or polymaths, embraced a proficient understanding of art, architecture, science, and engineering, leading to a period of wondrous discovery.

The Integration Report – Its Ideology

This ideology though, ignores division of knowledge in the Renaissance which was: liberal arts (people with true knowledge – Episteme) and the mechanical arts (people with Techne (e.g. the practical knowledge of the craftsmen). Or put another way, knowledge of the free people who think –Episteme – and the knowledge of those who use their hands and work – Techne. All very Ancient Greek in nature!

The statement in the *Collaborations of Consequence report* is also what sociologists refer to as knowledge – enough people believe it to make it more than just an idiosyncratic individual belief, but it is not what a philosopher would regard as knowledge – justified true belief. It is in fact an example of a socially constructed reality – a collection of beliefs, myths, false truth claims, misunderstandings, etc.

It is also an example of a scientific reduction to ignorance. More than that, it is a dangerous rewriting of history to make it fit with what people want that history to be. It is dangerous for many reasons, not least of which being, that this social construction of reality requires a significant rewrite of history per se, to make everything else fit with the quoted statement.

Whatever happened to the Enlightenment notion of scepticism towards people and organisations who speak with the voice of authority?

145

Unexpected Item in Bagging Area – Blake's Proverbs of Hell

From William Blake's *The Marriage of Heaven and Hell*:

The head Sublime, the heart Pathos, the genitals Beauty, the hands and feet Proportion.

As the air to a bird or the sea to a fish, so is contempt to the contemptible.

The crow wished every thing was black, the owl, that every thing was white.

Exuberance is Beauty.

If the lion was advised by the fox, he would be cunning.

Improvement makes strait roads, but the crooked roads without Improvement, are roads of Genius.

Sooner murder an infant in its cradle than nurse unacted desires.

Where man is not nature is barren.

Truth can never be told so as to be understood, and not be believed.

Enough! or Too much!

And Now Some Text is Analysed – 1

Not The Integration Report text, but an article entitled Look at The Leaders of Silicon Valley, updated August 3rd 2011, from The New York Times web site. When it was first published is not fully clear. Most likely late March 2011 (see why later).

As the title states it is an article about the Leaders – meaning people – of Silicon Valley.

Leaders means CEOs and heads of product engineering.

Is the article really about the Leaders of Silicon Valley, or something else?

The article's opening paragraph states: "It's commonly believed that engineers dominate Silicon Valley and that there is a correlation between capacity for innovation and an education in mathematics and the sciences. Both assumptions are false."

But what has this statement to do with the article, which does not address the disciplinary make-up of Silicon Valley, but a select group of people, claimed later in the article to be 652 in number, designated as Leaders?

Thus how can the author say that the assumption is false?

And Now Some Text is Analysed – 2

Self-evidently the author's statement that it is 'commonly believed' is itself an assumption! No evidence for this statement is evident!

Self-evidently the author's statement about the correlation is also an assumption! No evidence for this statement is provided either!

Is this paragraph just a (clumsy and thoughtless?) way of introducing the article, or is it carefully formulated to imply something?

Let's see! To do that we need to examine the second paragraph, which starts by stating: "My research team at Duke and Harvard surveyed 652 US-born CEOs and heads of product engineering at 502 technology companies."

He then goes on to say: "[...] 92% held bachelor's degrees, and 47% held higher degrees. But only 37% held degrees in engineering or computer technology, and just 2% held them in mathematics. The rest have degrees in fields as diverse as business, accounting, finance, healthcare, arts and the humanities."

Why, we ask, present the results like this?

And Now Some Text is Analysed – 3

We will now look at the results as they appear in the research as reported in a different genre of text – the research report.

And from that research report, we find that the survey is not of Silicon Valley companies, but just of engineering and technology companies listed in Dun and Bradstreet's (D&B) Million Dollar Database; companies founded in the period 1995-2005. The survey is of 652 U.S.-born tech founders from 502 of these engineering and technology companies. The response rate was approximately 40%, so that amounts to 261 individuals!

Of these 261 (not 652) individuals 47% held terminal degrees is STEM fields (computer science/information technology – 9%; mathematics – 2%; engineering – 28%; applied sciences – 8%).

Also, 33% of the 261 individuals held degrees in business, accounting and finance.

So 80% actually held degree qualifications in subjects relevant to running an engineering and technology company!

How many held a terminal degree in arts, humanities and social sciences? The answer is only 3%! This of course is not specifically mentioned in the article. Why?

And Now Some Text is Analysed – 4

So what we have learned is that 80% of the survey respondents – 261 people – held degrees relevant to running an engineering and technology business – 47% in STEM fields, 33% in business, finance or accounting.

And yet the third paragraph in the article states that: "Gaining a degree made a big difference in the sales and employment of the company that a founder started. But the field that the degree was in or the school it was obtained from was not a significant factor."

Oh really!

And what about the rest of the article?

The interest here is only the penultimate and final paragraphs:

"And then there is the matter of design. Steve Jobs taught the world that good engineering is important, but what matters the most is good design. You can teach artists how to use software and graphics tools, but it's much harder to turn engineers into artists.

"Our society needs liberal arts majors as much as engineers and scientists."

And Now Some Text is Analysed – 5

And now we reveal something that might explain ...

The analysed article is one of several published around March 21st 2011 under the theme Career Counselor: Bill Gates or Steve Jobs?

Why? Because The New York Times reports that "In a talk to the nation's governors earlier this month [March], Mr Gates emphasized work-related learning, arguing that education investment should be aimed at academic disciplines and departments that are 'well-correlated to areas that actually produce jobs.'"

The New York Times, then suggested that Steve Jobs was some advocate for liberal arts education, stating: "If this was not music to the ears of advocates of the humanities, they quickly found a soulmate in Steve Jobs. At an event unveiling new Apple products, Mr Jobs said: 'It's in Apple's DNA that technology alone is not enough – it's technology married with liberal arts, married with the humanities, that yields us the result that makes our heart sing and nowhere is that more true than in these post-PC devices."

Find if you can, any evidence that he was such an advocate. We have looked and found nothing. We did though find something, but not what people are assuming they might find!

Steve Jobs Quoted in Full

"So, I've said this before, I though that it was worth repeating. It's in Apple's DNA that technology alone is not enough, that it's technology married with liberal arts, married with the humanities, that yields us the result that make our heart sing, and nowhere is that more true than in these post-PC devices. And a lot of folks in the Tablet market are rushing in and they're looking at this as the next PC. The hardware and the software are done by different companies, and they're talking about speeds and feeds just like they did with PCs. And our experience and every bone in our bodies says that is not the right approach to this, that these are post-PC devices that need to be even easier to use than a PC. They need to be even more intuitive than a PC, and where the software and the hardware and the applications need to intertwine in an even more seamless way than they do on a PC. And we think we're on the right track with this. We think that we have the right architecture, not just in silicon, but in the organisation to build these kinds of products. And so I think we stand a pretty good chance of being pretty competitive in this market and I hope that what you see today gives you a good feel for that."

Steve Jobs, iPad2 Launch Event, March 2011

152

Steve Jobs Quoted Again

"I think our major contribution [to computing] was in bringing a liberal arts point of view to the use of computers. If you really look at the ease of use of the Macintosh, the driving motivation behind that was to bring not only ease of use to people — so that many, many more people could use computers for nontraditional things at that time — but it was to bring beautiful fonts and typography to people, it was to bring graphics to people ... so that they could see beautiful photographs, or pictures, or artwork, etc ... to help them communicate. ... Our goal was to bring a liberal arts perspective and a liberal arts audience to what had traditionally been a very geeky technology and a very geeky audience."

Steve Jobs' 1996 Conversation With Terry Gross

Steve Jobs Quoted One More Time

"In my perspective ... science and computer science is a liberal art, it's something everyone should know how to use, at least, and harness in their life. It's not something that should be relegated to 5 percent of the population over in the corner. It's something that everybody should be exposed to and everyone should have mastery of to some extent, and that's how we viewed computation and these computation devices."

Steve Jobs' 1996 Conversation With Terry Gross

Apple and their Liberal Arts Perspective on Computing – It's all in the Architecture

That would be the organisational architecture ...

Behind Steve Jobs, was that which it seems no one has bothered to look at – Apple's design studio. It is closed, like the rest of Apple, but we do know who has led Apple's design work – Jonathon Ive, Apple's Chief Design Officer.

According to Apple's web site, Ive is responsible for all design at Apple, including the look and feel of Apple hardware, user interface, packaging, major architectural projects such as Apple Park and Apple's retail stores, as well as new ideas and future initiatives. He has led Apple's design team, which is widely regarded as one of the world's best.

And what sort of expertise does Apple's design studio use? That cannot be seen, but you can get a good idea by looking at the composition of skills at Philips Design in the Netherlands.

At Philips Design You Will Find ...

Here is a list disciplines as defined by the qualification of members of staff:

Cultural Anthropology and a Minor in Fine Art

Visual Communication

BA (Hons) Graphic Design

BA (Hons) Visual Communication

Multimedia and Communication Design

Industrial Design

Design Engineering

User-System Interaction

Design for Industry

Mobility

Behavioural Science and Digital Media

Media and Communication

Industrial Design Engineering

Applied Arts

Industrial Product Design

Fashion Design

Graphic Information Design

Design Management

Communications and Commercial Economy

Interior Decoration

Culture, Organization and Management

Marketing and Management

Brand Experience Design

Photography

Contemporary Art

Biology

Architecture, Urban Planning and Design

New Media

Design Driven Companies

Those that, to consumer markets do orientate, most likely would be, design driven companies these days, if to be successful is their aim. Design is a competitive edge, and in the organisational architecture is where this thinking should be embedded.

Our list of those companies that we suspect are design driven: Apple (and their serious competitors), Laura Ashley, BMW (and other automotive companies), Ikea, Habitat, Wedgwood, Dyson, Kenwood (and other appliance manufacturers) ...

And if you want to know what modern design is about, we suggest you read a blog, posted in 2010, by a design guru called Professor Donald Norman. The title is: Why Design Education Must Change.

Any of these design related issues discussed in The Integration Report? Could be useful for STEM educators to know! Could be useful for Engineering Institutions to know given their role in accrediting engineering degree courses!

Of course they are not discussed!

A FT Journalist Gets his Facts Wrong!

In February 2016 a FT journalist (FT's executive comment editor) wrote, in an article called *Degrees of Separation*:

"In 2008, researchers at Duke and Harvard universities asked 652 US-born chief executives and heads of product engineering at technology companies about their education. Unsurprisingly, most of those surveyed were highly educated but only 37 percent had graduated in engineering or computer science, and a paltry 2 percent had qualified in maths. The rest — around two-thirds — had degrees in a wide range of subjects, from the arts and humanities, to business, finance and healthcare.... "

You now know of course that strictly this not correct, because only 261 individuals responded and 55% had a degree in a STEM subject.

The article was about the STEM vs Liberal Arts Education debate!

So when we say that misinformation is everywhere, we are highlighting a growing problem with people in authority, as well as a more general problem!

In the USA, Liberal Arts Education is Under Attack!

The previously mentioned FT journalist also wrote, in the article called Degrees of Separation: "Three years later, Bill Gates, the founder of Microsoft, made a speech to US state governors calling for more investment in STEM subjects (science, technology, engineering and maths). He argued that the US was falling behind other countries in these fields, which were 'well correlated to areas that actually produce jobs'."

Several publications, around March 2011, reported this speech. It kicked-off a defensive debate as well as accusations of elitism – directed towards liberal arts educators and colleges engaged in defending liberal arts.

The publisher's summary of Fareed Zakaria's 2015 book, In Defence of Liberal Arts Education, states: "The governors of Florida, Texas and North Carolina have all pledged that they will not spend taxpayer money subsidizing the liberal arts ..."

Is this attack on liberal arts education mentioned in The Integration Report? No! But now you know a little more about the context of the report ...

And the claim – the defensive claim – of the liberal arts education establishment is that a liberal arts education teaches you how to think. Which quite an elitist claim and which leads us to CP Snow ...

Unexpected Item in Bagging Area – Edmund Burke Speaks

Edmund Burke will now speak:

"Because half a dozen grasshoppers under a fern make the field ring with their importunate chink, whilst thousands of great cattle, reposed beneath the shadow of the British oak, chew the cud and are silent, pray do not imagine that those who make the noise are the only inhabitants of the field; that, of course, they are many in number, or that, after all, they are other than the little, shrivelled, meagre, hopping, though loud and troublesome, insects of the hour."

Below is a Japanese maple leaf!

CP Snow and the Free People who Think, and the Slaves who Work!

There is an old adage which represents how the Ancient Greeks looked at the world: free people think, slaves work. This is what underlies F W Taylor's so called Scientific Management: the free people (managers) think, the slaves (manual workers) work.

In Taylor's words: "Under our system [of management] the workman is told minutely just what he is to do and how he is to do it; and any improvement which he makes upon the orders given him is fatal to success."

In the world that CP Snow knew, the elitist world of classically educated government civil servants of the 1930s, 1940s and 1950s, he would have encountered this Ancient Greek mindset in this form:

Free people – the liberal arts / classically educated – think, the slaves – the applied scientists and vocationally educated – work.

Hence his polemic, and the two cultures rhetoric – surely you don't think he really thought that there were two cultures?

CP Snow and *The Integration Report*

CP Snow's two cultures gets a mention in *The Integration Report*. What is the probability that CP Snow's words have been accurately quoted?

Usually he is misquoted! *The Integration Report* says that, in 1959 C. P. Snow famously lamented that the divisions between the sciences and the arts and humanities, which he described as "two cultures," were a rift of our own making. The report then quotes Snow as saying that the intellectual life of the whole of western society is increasingly being split into two polar groups.

The Integration Report also states that C.P. Snow was a British Scientist and novelist who in his 1959 Rede Lecture described a gap between the sciences and humanities.

Are these statements correct? Or are people reading into texts what they want to read? Let us look at the facts that can be extracted from the texts found in *The Integration Report*.

CP Snow and The Integration Report

The facts are:

1. In 1959 C. P. Snow famously lamented that the divisions between the sciences and the arts and humanities were a rift of our own making.

2. This he said was a gap between the sciences and the humanities.

3. He described this division as two cultures.

4. He wrote that the intellectual life of the whole of western society is increasingly being split into two polar groups.

5. CP Snow was a British scientists and novelist.

So these are the 5 facts that you are armed with as a result of reading The Integration Report. Very probably you will not question these. You will just accept them.

Only, most of the above 5 facts are highly inaccurate, even misleading, and could be seen as misinformation.

Time to analyse CP Snow's texts!

CP Snow and The Integration Report

This is what CP Snow actually wrote in the text of his 1959 Rede Lecture:

"I believe the intellectual life of the whole of western society is increasingly being split into two polar groups. When I say the intellectual life, I mean to include also a large part of our practical life, because I should be the last person to suggest the two can at the deepest level be distinguished. I shall come back to the practical life a little later. Two polar groups: at one pole we have the literary intellectuals, who incidentally while no one was looking took to referring to themselves as 'intellectuals' as though there were no others. I remember G. H. Hardy once remarking to me in mild puzzlement, some time in the 1930s: 'Have you noticed how the word intellectual is used nowadays? There seems to be a new definition which certainly doesn't include Rutherford or Eddington or Dirac or Adrian or me. It does seem rather odd, don't y' know.'

"Literary intellectuals at one pole — at the other scientists, and as the most representative, the physical scientists. Between the two a gulf of mutual incomprehension — sometimes (particularly among the young) hostility and dislike, but most of all lack of understanding ... "

CP Snow and The Integration Report

Time now for quick CP Snow biography, because few people ever mention this – it is contextual!

Snow received a vocational higher education – in physics. He undertook research in (reportedly) molecular physics. Then, disastrously, a highly acclaimed published paper that he co-authored was found to contain an error and the paper was retracted. This signalled the end of his scientific career. He said later that he did not have enthusiasm for science, his passion being writing. His third published novel appeared in 1934. This is about a scientist who published material that is found to be incorrect, and who then gives up science and becomes a writer! His third novel was (according to Snow) a partial success. Later Snow became involved with the British civil service, ending up as a Civil Service Commissioner. Much later still, he was involved in government, as a Minister. By the time his New Statesman Two Cultures article was published in 1956, he had not been an active scientist for over 20 years.

CP Snow was a novelist, a civil servant, a politician, and a man with a mission.

CP Snow and The Integration Report

And what was that mission ? It was certainly not to
bridge the so-called two cultures gap. Being involved in
government, during the Second World War, and in the
post war years, Snow would have been acutely aware of
the central importance of science and technology both to
defence and to economic growth. And yet he would
have also encountered an establishment that was deeply
ignorant of both science and technology. He would also
have known that there was a need for those in
government to become scientifically and technologically
literate. Probably he recognised, like many in the
1950s, that science and technology were the future,
and that what we now call STEM people, were
becoming central to economic and political decision
making – the emergence of what, in the late 1960s,
was called by the French sociologist, Alain Touraine, the
post-industrial society.

Two cultures is rhetoric and the clues lie in several texts,
most of which are very rarely (if ever) mentioned by
those who refer to Snow and the two cultures. That
would be people on both sides of the so-called divide;
STEM and those who are in the arts and humanities
(or liberal arts if you use that term).

Why is this important to know this? Wait. Soon you will
find out!

CP Snow and *The Integration Report*

We have undertaken a word analysis of the texts of the 1956 *New Statesman* article, the 1959 *Rede Lecture* and the 1963/64 follow-up called *The Cultures: A Second Look*. It is very revealing. No where in these texts does he mention humanities. He only mentions artists 4 times – quite a revelation as many of these people seem to be convinced that he was talking about a separation between art and science. Different area of activity, different interpretation!

He mentions art or arts 17 times. But how many times does he mention science or scientists, engineering or engineers, mathematics or mathematicians, industry or industrial or industrialisation or industrialise. A lot is the answer:

Science – 66 times; scientist(s) – 113 times; engineering – 9 times; engineer(s) – 19 times; industry – 14 times; industrial etc. – 55 times; technology – 6 times; mathematics – 8 times; mathematician(s) – 3 times.

He mentions literature 20 times, literary 50 times, and writer(s) 24 times.

This data is a pointer. Note the emphasis on what we now call STEM. Note the total neglect of humanities. Note the scant attention to art and artists. Note the emphasis on literary people – writers.

CP Snow on the matter of Writers and Auschwitz!

Now for something that those (elitist?) liberal arts people and artists never mention and that is the linking, in the Rede Lecture, of writers and Auschwitz. Obviously it is not mentioned in The Integration Report!

On page 7, Snow mentions what a scientist of distinction said to him: "[...] Yeats, Pound, Wyndham Lewis, nine out of ten of those who have dominated literary sensibility in our time – weren't they not only politically silly, but politically wicked? Didn't the influence of all they represent bring Auschwitz that much nearer?"

And in response Snow says: "I thought at the time, and I still think, that the correct answer was not to defend the indefensible. [...] It was no use defying the facts, which are broadly true. The honest answer was that there is, in fact, a connection, which literary persons were culpably slow to see, between some kinds of early twentieth-century art and the most imbecile expressions of anti-social feeling [...].

And there is also a connection between artists and the development of the totalitarian Soviet regime, with the same imbecilic ideas that contributed to this, now rolled-out again in the European Union in an activity known as STARTS.

The Two Cultures – A Gross Oversimplification

"I have been argued with by non-scientists of strong down-to-earth interests. Their view is that it is an over-simplification, and that if one is going to talk in these terms there ought to be at least three cultures. They argue that, though they are not scientists themselves, they would share a good deal of the scientific feeling. They would have as little use – perhaps, since they knew more about it, even less use – for the recent literary culture as the scientists themselves. J. H. Plumb, Alan Bullock and some of my American sociological friends have said that they vigorously refuse to be corralled in a cultural box with people they wouldn't be seen dead with, or to be regarded as helping to produce a climate which would not permit of social hope.

"I respect those arguments. The number 2 is a very dangerous number: that is why the dialectic is a dangerous process. Attempts to divide anything into two ought to be regarded with much suspicion. I have thought a long time about going in for further refinements: but in the end I have decided against. I was searching for something a little more than a dashing metaphor, a good deal less than a cultural map: and for those purposes the two cultures is about right. And subtilising any more would bring more disadvantages than it's worth."

The Two Cultures – A Gross Oversimplification

Later, after much criticism, Snow admitted to the existence of a third culture, perhaps because the notion of two cultures is indeed a gross over simplification.

In the text of his first novel – The Search – he deals with differences among the cultures of different disciplines, not just the difference between the discipline of economics and the natural sciences, but cultural differences among the natural sciences.

Each discipline is a culture unto itself. The differences among engineering disciplines shows this clearly. CP Snow demonstrates awareness of this in his writings, in one case mentioning engineers (not in a very complementary way) in comparison to natural scientists. Why then did he persist with this notion of two cultures?

Evidently he is directing his venom towards one group, and one group alone – the so called literary intellectuals of his era. No where does he single out any other discipline, or group. He refers only to literary intellectuals. The two cultures rhetoric is the device he uses to do that, but why?

You will not find the answer in the three, two cultures texts we mentioned and analysed, but elsewhere.

The New Culture – Scientists in Government

"I want scientists active in all levels of government. By
scientists I mean people trained in the natural sciences,
not only engineers, though I want them too. But I
want a special requirement for the scientist proper,
because, partly by training, partly by self-selection,
they include a number of speculative and socially
imaginative minds. While engineers – more uniform in
attitude than one would expect a professional class to be
– tend to be technically bold and advanced but, at the
same time to accept totally any society into which they
may have happened to be born. The scientist proper are
nothing like so homogeneous in attitude, and some of
them will provide a quality which it seems to me we
need above everything else. [...] In my view, and it is
one of the points from which I started, it would be a
real gain. It is a clear advantage to the Soviet Union
that they have, right at the top of the political and
administrative trees, a fairly high proportion of men
with scientific or technical training."

So from one elite – liberal arts – to another elite –
vocationally educated scientists – yet another group,
with people deeply implicated in authoritarian and
totalitarian regimes, as well as actively contributing to
'paving the way to Auschwitz'.

CP Snow and *The Integration Report*

Why is all this important? We return to the question posed earlier (p. 166)! The answer: Because the free people do not think, not at least in the way that they might believe. We refer you here to the work of the Nobel prize winning cognitive psychologist, Daniel Kahneman.

Two cultures illustrates the point. It has taken on a life of its own and is accepted without thinking 'slowly'. It is a belief that has become knowledge in the sociological sense, but not in the philosophical sense of justified true belief. It is unquestioned. To question it, is heretical. People just accept it, as a learned assumption, that CP Snow was referring to ... What depends on where you stand, which socially constructed reality you subscribe to. The reasoning goes like this: Snow is evidently talking about a rift, which people then start to reason exists, finding the evidence that they want to find that supports that belief, ignoring the evidence that does not – like Snow's reference to people who are non-scientists that do not identify with – the literary intellectuals (at that far pole) that Snow has specifically identified as being worthy of our scorn. Yes he wants us to join with him in condemning these literary intellectuals. Recall that its a polemic ...

Thus do we make a comment about ...

Let there be Light, and there was Light!

Thus do we make a comment about a statement in The Integration Report, where no thinking, critical or otherwise is evident. The statement in question refers to a specific example (of integration) where, it is claimed, students who applied their scientific understanding of light to create artistic products could also use their visual aids as a way to communicate scientific ideas and findings, creating an artistic-scientific loop that contributes to creative thinking and the ability to deal with complex problems innovatively. A paper, Shen et al., (2015) is then referenced.

Oh really! Is this claim accurate? We will check to see if this is correct! We investigated the statement by referring to the reference Shen et al. (2015). If you do what we did, you will find nothing in that reference that would lead you to make the statement that can be found in The Integration Report!

The full details of the reference are (it is a book chapter): Shen, J., S. Jiang, and O. L. Liu. 2015. Reconceptualizing a college science learning experience in the new digital era: A review of literature. pp. 61-79 in Emerging Technologies for STEAM Education: Full Steam Ahead, X. Ge, D. Ifenthaler, and J. Spector, eds. Cham, Switzerland: Springer.

Let there be Light, and there was Light!

The paper by Shen et al., (2015) is a short literature review that examines technology as an instructional support for the development of life-long learning skills. It also addresses the matter of technology-enriched assessment of the development of life-long learning skills.

In the section that deals with technology resources the paper reviews five types of technological resource: Personal response system (i.e., Clickers); Computer visualizations and simulations (CVS), including virtual labs; Computer supported collaborative learning (CSCL), including online discussion and social networks; Educational video & computer games (VCG); and Open Course Ware (OCW) & MOOCs.

For reasons that are not immediately self-evident, in the technological resources section, included is a non-technological resource – Connection to Arts. The reason for this may be linked to the title of the book! In other words the authors may just have added this material to make the work fit with the theme of the book which is – STEAM!

174

Let there be Light, and there was Light!

What is said is this section *Connection to Arts*? Here is a summary: It is stated that efforts have been made to connect science education with art education because arts practices can promote inspiration and interests. They then very briefly refer to three examples, not giving much in the way of detail.

In the first case considered the provided web link is no longer operational. The example has something to do with developing curricular materials that integrate mathematics, science, computer science, and digital sound production. What exactly is not clear. The second example relates to light (as mentioned in *The Integration Report*). We will deal with this separately.

The third example, is software that can help practicing scientists to create and animate 3-D molecules and hence communicate information. Little is said beyond this. It is supposed to be an example of linking arts and sciences to exploit the power of visualisation. Is it? Sounds more like computer-aided ... Also mentioned at the end is a competition hosted by *Science Magazine* called *Dance Your Phd*.

The closing words of this short, brief and (to be very honest) not very informative part of the chapter, the authors say: "Despite these innovative approaches, however, research on connecting arts and science at the college level still needs much empirical work."

Let there be Light, and there was Light!

What is said in the second example that relates to light? This:

"Sciences and arts can support each other for students to learn science concepts. For example, Bopegedera (2005) conducted a light-related program in which students participated in both art workshops and science labs in order to help students to use scientific understanding of light to create artistic products. In the art workshops students could draw and paint products by hand or using graphing software (e.g., constructing light waves with yarn), while in the science labs students could learn concepts related to light (e.g., the relationships among frequency, wavelength, and the speed of light)."

So where in the above is mention of students who apply their scientific understanding of light to create artistic products could also use their visual aids as a way to communicate scientific ideas and findings, creating an artistic–scientific loop that contributes to creative thinking and the ability to deal with complex problems innovatively?

Notice mention of the reference Bopegedera (2005), which is not mentioned in The Integration Report. What is in this reference? We obtained it and found ...

Let there be Light, and there was Light!

Bopegedera (2005), full title of the paper is: *The Art and Science of Light – An Interdisciplinary Teaching and Learning Experience*. These are the key points – the things that did not find their way into the paper by Shen et al., (2015):

Almost all the students who enrolled on the course were arts majors;

It is a programme – a full time course load for the duration, providing immersion in a topic for a significant period of time;

It was structured – in the first quarter the focus was on skill building in lab sciences, art studio, and library research methods.

Each week students attended lectures, workshops, seminars, science labs, art studio work & discussion sessions (students' work was displayed & critiqued).

It is a rejection of approaches used to teach chemistry students which involves solving problems using mathematical relationships – for students who had avoided science most of their lives, this approach was not appropriate.

This is an effective way of teaching science to non-science students thereby hooking them into science.

Let there be Light, and there was Light!

So as regards the claim in The Integration Report, that, as a specific example (of integration), students who apply their scientific understanding of light to create artistic products could also use their visual aids as a way to communicate scientific ideas and findings, creating an artistic–scientific loop that contributes to creative thinking and the ability to deal with complex problems innovatively (Shen et al., 2015), we invite you to insert below the word, words or phrase that best expresses your views on these types of claims that bear no relation to the actual case:

. . . .

Let there be Light, and there was Light!

We were not surprised by what we found! There are several examples like this in *The Integration Report*, and other reports too that engage in arts advocacy, or arts/humanities advocacy. It has, sadly, become the norm!

Why?

We suppose you must have guessed already …

That which *STARTS* to *STEAM* is an attempt by some artists and arts organisations to transfer themselves from the dingy ghetto of restricted arts funding to the relatively opulent palaces of *STEM* funding. Or in the case of liberal arts advocacy reports, to do something similar …

And that is the fundamental reason why these advocacy reports are created – they are creations.

And what of the golden threads? Well obviously you should not ask those that think – or perhaps we should say, those who think that they think – what these are.

Unexpected Item in Bagging Area – Beauty will Save the World

Alexandr Solzhenitsyn will now speak:

"So perhaps the old trinity of Truth, Goodness, and Beauty is not simply the decorous and antiquated formula it seemed to us at the time of our self-confident materialistic youth. If the tops of these three trees do converge, as thinkers used to claim, and if the all too obvious and the overly straight sprouts of Truth and Goodness have been crushed, cut down, or not permitted to grow, then perhaps the whimsical, unpredictable, and ever surprising shoots of Beauty will force their way through and soar up to that very spot, thereby fulfilling the task of all three.

"And then no slip of the tongue but a prophecy would be contained in Dostoyevsky's words: 'Beauty will save the world.'

"Countries and entire continents continually repeat each other's mistakes with a time lag – occasionally one of centuries – when, it would seem, everything is so very clear. But no: What one people has already endured, appraised, and rejected suddenly emerges among another people as the very latest word. Here once again the sole substitute for an experience which we have not ourselves lived through is art and literature. Both are endowed with the miraculous power to communicate – despite differences in language, custom, and social structure – the experience of the entire nation to another nation which has not undergone such a difficult decades long collective experience. In a fortunate instance, this could save an entire nation from a redundant, or erroneous, or even destructive course, thereby shortening the tortuous paths of human history."

And Another Example – 1

The *Integration Report* mentions that there is a study that examined Michigan State University Honours College science and technology graduates from the period 1990–1995. This study made several claims. It claimed that STEM majors are far more likely to have extensive arts and crafts skills than the average American. It also asserted that arts and crafts experiences are significantly correlated with producing patentable inventions and founding new companies. Additionally it stated that the majority of survey respondents believed that their innovative ability has been stimulated by their arts and crafts knowledge. And it declared that lifelong participation and exposure in the arts and crafts yields significant impacts for innovators and entrepreneurs

Sorry but, if you had been thinking critically you would have seen and reported that the paper referred to (LaMore et al., 2013) says that the results may be biased – a self selection bias. And if you had taken a look at the sample question mentioned in the paper, critical thinking would have led you to see that there is also, possibly, a response bias as well, because the question is not worded to avoid response bias.

And Another Example – 2

The *Integration Report* also mentions a comparative study of an undergraduate neuroscience course. This particular study, The Integration Report, claims, found that students who were required to apply their understanding of neurotransmission through the creative activity of making a 3- to 5-minute film significantly outperformed those who learned the concept from more conventional approaches. It is also claimed that the authors of the study found that this learning transcended several levels of Bloom's revised taxonomy. In addition, The Integration Report claims, students who participated in the integrative assignments reported that, while it was challenging to simplify the process of neurotransmission into a video, they felt more confident in their ability to apply neurotransmission in future classes. The process of creating helped them, it is said, to reduce the complexity of the scientific concept to its most salient features.

Sorry but if you had been thinking critically you would have seen that this case study (Jarvinen and Jarvinen, 2012) is not an example of integration of arts and humanities into the academic programme of students majoring in STEM! It is an example of an experimental technology-aided teaching exercise.

More details follow ...

And Another Example – 3

Jarvinen and Jarvinen (2012) report: "Students who were required to apply their understanding of neurotransmission through the creation of a video significantly outperformed those who learned the concept from more conventional approaches."

A critical thinker however would have noted that the Materials and Methods section states that all the students undertaking the video project (VID), had already undertaken the compulsory group PowerPoint (PPT) project, all of whom had also undertaken the compulsory Conventional Approach (CA) (i.e. lectures) which also involved group work among the students.

The clarity (and banality) of the research is seen in another paper by these authors, where two groups making videos are compared: "the scientific method (SM) group performed significantly better on scientific method assessment questions, the neurotransmission (NT) group performed significantly better on neurotransmission questions, and the SM and NT groups performed similarly on concepts not assigned in the video project."
Which can be summarised as: once (CA) good, twice (CA + PPT) better, three times (CA+PPT+VID) even better.

This example looks like a case study in Active Learning!

Active Learning – 1

Is active learning mentioned in *The Integration Report*? Not much! Twice actually, and in both cases with reference to a paper (Olds and Miller, 2004), which is another supposed example of integration of arts and humanities into the academic programme of students majoring in STEM. Is it? We will return to that matter.

Active learning is mentioned (twice) in another National Academies report, with the title the *Graduate STEM Education for the 21ˢᵗ Century*.

The first mention refers to research on undergraduate education which has demonstrated that using effective pedagogical practices, such as active learning, increases student learning and retention.

The second mention states that while there has been increased attention to the pedagogy and practice in effective STEM undergraduate education, which includes critical components of active learning, blended classrooms, and discipline-based education research, there is a relatively smaller proportion of educational research targeted toward understanding effective models and practices in graduate education.

But to what extent is active learning already built into STEM courses? No answer is to be found in either report. Which is surprising because ...

Active Learning – 2

Active learning was identified as being important ...

We introduce now another report – not mentioned in The Integration Report – the report entitled: Engage to Excel: Producing One Million Additional College Graduates with Degrees in Science, Technology, Engineering, and Mathematics. It is the report published in 2012 by the President's Council of Advisors on Science and Technology's STEM Undergraduate Working Group:

"Learning theory, empirical evidence about how people learn, and assessment of outcomes in STEM classrooms all point to a need to improve teaching methods to enhance learning and student persistence. Classroom approaches that engage students in active learning improve retention of information and critical thinking skills, compared with a sole reliance on lecturing, and increase persistence of students in STEM majors."

Why our focus on active learning?

What The Integration Report Did Not Say ...

In the US, the National Survey of Student Engagement's (Former) Benchmarks of Effective Educational Practice (2011 Report): Active and Collaborative Learning

"Students learn more when they are intensely involved in their education and are asked to think about and apply what they are learning in different settings. Collaborating with others in solving problems or mastering difficult material prepares students to deal with the messy, unscripted problems they will encounter daily, both during and after college."

Benchmark measures:

- Asked questions in class or contributed to class discussions
- Made a class presentation
- Worked with other students on projects during class
- Worked with classmates outside of class to prepare class assignments
- Tutored or taught other students (paid or voluntary)
- Participated in a community-based project (e.g., service-learning) as part of a regular course
- Discussed ideas from readings or classes with others outside of class (students, family members, co-workers, etc.).

Benchmarks have now been replaced with Engagement Indicators, one of which is (2017 Report): Reflective & Integrative Learning.

And The Integration Report Says …

The Integration Report says that a review of the published literature was undertaken which revealed that a disproportionate number of articles on integrative graduate study framed interdisciplinary graduate work as a proxy for participation in interdisciplinary courses (Meyer et al., 2016; Newswander and Borrego, 2009; Posselt et al., 2017) or on interdisciplinary research teams (Borrego and Cutler, 2010; Borrego and Newswander, 2010; Hackett and Rhoten, 2009; Newswander and Borrego, 2009; Rhoten et al., 2009). The Integration Report says that, as a result, and due to the lack of rigorous research designs, many of the lessons extracted from the empirical articles on interdisciplinary work reflect an emphasis on working on interdisciplinary teams, rather than on exposure to and participation in interdisciplinary graduate experiences.

Oh really! Should we check? Let us see, for example, what Borrego and Newswander (2010) actually said!

What *The Integration Report* did Not Say ...

This is what Borrego and Newswander (2010) actually said about their analysis of 130 IGERT proposals, using an approach that coded the content most directly related to transferable interdisciplinary student learning outcomes into four categories: (a) grounding in traditional disciplines; (b) integration and broad perspectives; (c) teamwork; and (d) interdisciplinary communication.

And this is what they found:

50% of proposals described ways in which graduate students would develop knowledge and awareness of multiple traditional disciplines in order to conduct interdisciplinary research.

30% of proposals emphasised some sort of systems thinking or integration of this knowledge from multiple disciplines.

41% articulated teamwork as an interdisciplinary learning outcome.

24% described interdisciplinary communication as a goal or outcome, as a professional development outcome, which also included in some cases diversity issues and ethics.

So exposure to and participation in interdisciplinary graduate experiences, or not? Answer according to your beliefs, ideology, vested interests ...

What, *The Integration Report*, did Not, Say ...

Reasons why teamwork appears in many interdisciplinary graduate research schemes:

- Because teamwork is already an established way of working, especially in STEM fields;

- Because teamwork is an established way of undertaking interdisciplinary work;

- Because teamwork is a 21st century skill – according to *The Integration Report!*

- Because, according to the NSF (2009) report, *Impact of Transformative Interdisciplinary Research and Graduate Education on Academic Institutions*: "Teamwork skills are a necessity for all graduate students regardless of their graduate programs." and

- "90 percent of IGERT graduates employed in the workforce reported that they regularly work as part of a team in their current jobs. As for their level of preparation for working on a team, 47 percent reported that their graduate programs prepared them 'very well,' 42 percent reported they were prepared 'well,' and 11 percent reported that their graduate programs did not prepare them well for this."

The final words go to Borrego and Newswander (2010), who are quoted out of context for the purpose of rhetoric: "[...] humanities emphasised (solitary) intellectual skills, whereas science and engineering emphasised interpersonal skills [...]."

And The Integration Report Says ...

The Integration Report says that many of the lessons extracted from the empirical articles on interdisciplinary work reflect an emphasis on working on interdisciplinary teams, rather than on exposure to and participation in interdisciplinary graduate experiences.

It also say that criticisms of this approach have questioned the use of work on interdisciplinary teams as the primary means for enacting interdisciplinary graduate practice: specifically, authors have cautioned that this emphasis may reinforce the mindset that more disciplines is better (Strengers, 2014, p. 550), overemphasize problem-based learning in interdisciplinary work (Stentoft, 2017), and neglect the nuances associated with how individuals solve interdisciplinary problems within interdisciplinary teams (Zhang and Shen, 2015).

Oh really! Should we check and see what the above reference actually say? Yes of course we will ...

What *The Integration Report* did not say ...

According to *The Integration Report*, Strengers, (2014, p. 550) says that authors have cautioned that this emphasis may ... reinforce the mindset that more disciplines is better

What did Strengers actually say on p.550? This:

"As an interdisciplinary researcher, I can sympathise with this view [that theoretical and applied interdisciplinary research will be necessary to solve entwined issues of social, environmental and economic sustainability] but am concerned about the lack of critical attention it has received from the academic community, particularly the assumption embedded in such claims that 'more' (disciplines) is better. The increasingly common call to break down disciplinary boundaries and work towards a common goal is one which Evans and Marvin (2006, p.1012) have warned is 'deceptively simple'. They caution against the 'methodological naivety' of assuming that 'more disciplines lead to more complete knowledge as the gaps and lacunae of one group are filled and completed by the skills and knowledge of others' (Evans and Marvin (2006, p1012)."

What *The Integration Report* did not say ...

Strengers (2014, p. 550) continued ...

"Interdisciplinary research is particularly challenging for the doctoral candidate, who may not yet have firm foundations within their own discipline while being asked to collaborate and integrate with others. Consider for example O'Reilly's (2009, p220) call for sociologists to adopt a 'disciplined sociology' or 'a position on firm ground' before they embark upon interdisciplinary research. This is a challenging task for the doctoral candidate who is in training to become a sociologist, as opposed to a sociologist who is training to become an interdisciplinary researcher. They must become a master of their own discipline, as well as others.

Um! Yes we see. So, it is not that the use of work on interdisciplinary teams as the primary means for enacting interdisciplinary graduate practice, is a problem per se, but that there is a tension between focusing on one's own discipline, and trying at the same time to develop interdisciplinary skills. And that, ironically, interdisciplinarity may lead, as a necessity, to reinforcement of a single disciplinary focus – you will have to read O'Reilly's paper to understand the last point!

But what did Evans and Marvin say?

What The Integration Report did not say ...

Evans and Marvin (2006, p.1012) actually said:

"The case for interdisciplinary work on the urban environment is deceptively simple: sustainability is a complex problem that transcends conventional disciplines and requires the social, engineering, and natural sciences each to contribute their relevant expertise. As such, sustainable-city research is an ideal site for examining interdisciplinarity in practice and thus, in passing, also to shed some light on wider developments in social science literatures in which, for example, the limits of scientific worldviews are emphasised and the need for increasingly diverse and heterogeneous forums for developing knowledge are promoted. Examples of these approaches include [...] ecological modernisation [...] reflexive modernisation [...] postnormal science constructive technology assessment [...] mode 1 and mode 2 forms of knowledge production, and [...] articulation.

"The implications of these perspectives is that ...

What The Integration Report did not say ...

Evans and Marvin (2006, p.1012) said:

"The implication of these perspectives is that contemporary social and environmental problems demand a community of all the experts, in which `expert' is defined increasingly broadly, and in which the different experiences, knowledges, and politics are all included in an integrated, holistic, approach to a complex problem or set of problems. For example, if it is the case that scientific knowledge of the sort produced by the research councils is more accurately understood as the knowledge of a particular social group (that is, scientists) within a disciplinary tradition, and not as an epistemologically superior understanding of the world, then the reasons for excluding other groups diminish (see, for example, Collins and Evans, 2002; Irwin and Michael, 2003). From these viewpoints, more disciplines lead to more complete knowledge as the gaps and lacunae of one group are filled and complemented by the skills and knowledge of the others.

"There is, however, a problem with this ...

What, The Integration Report, did not, say ...

Evans and Marvin (2006, p.1012) actually said:

"There is, however, a problem with this approach. Its implicit assumption is that it is possible to triangulate between the various theories and methods that different disciplines bring to the problem. In effect, the assumption is that, there is just one problem and that, by approaching it from many different sides, we can build up a complete picture. Taken to its limit, this would suggest a return to the `unity of science' movement proposed by the logical positivists but, even if the claims are not that strong, the idea of triangulation is nonetheless problematic. On the one hand, there are concerns coming from more constructivist perspectives, such as science and technology studies (Jasanoff et al, 1995), where there is considerable sympathy for Wittgenstein (1953) and Winch (1958), and Kuhn's (1996) idea of a scientific paradigm, as well as from the broader range of cultural, feminist, postcolonial, and other studies linked to the idea of standpoint epistemology. It is not necessary to be a radical or critical social scientist to raise the concerns, however. The problems of triangulation are also the stuff of undergraduate research methods texts (for example, Bryman, 2004) and there are, therefore, many reasons to be cautious about the progressive rhetoric of interdisciplinarity."

What *The Integration Report* did not say ...

If you take a critical look, you will soon realise that *The Integration Report* is built on the assumption that it is possible to triangulate between the various theories and methods that different disciplines bring to a problem, because they are all branches of the same tree.

That's the underlying belief, and its essentially a *Unity of Knowledge* belief. A socially constructed reality.

But, if you look you will find that often it is not possible to integrate, because of epistemological and ontological incompatibilities.

And so the world of the art-science lovers falls apart! Who among them will ever know, such is their detachment from the reality of justified true beliefs!

What The Integration Report did not say ...

The Integration Report claims that Stentoft (2017) says
that criticisms of this approach have questioned the use
of work on interdisciplinary teams as the primary
means for enacting interdisciplinary graduate practice:
specifically, authors have cautioned that this emphasis
may ... overemphasize problem-based learning in
interdisciplinary work.

What did Stentoft actually say? This:

"Problem-based learning (PBL) is often characterised as a
pedagogical approach offering possibilities for students
to engage in interdisciplinary learning. Rather than
supporting content learning of a single discipline, the
problem-based approach puts the problem to be solved
before the 'tools to solve it', and this, as is suggested,
opens up to transgressing disciplinary boundaries in the
search for solutions. At a first glance, a problem-based
pedagogy therefore appears a compelling response to the
challenges of developing a curriculum where
interdisciplinary learning is encouraged and adequately
scaffolded. However, a comprehensive understanding of
how PBL may be organised to scaffold interdisciplinary
learning has yet to be fully developed.

"There is consequently ...

What *The Integration Report* did not say ...

Stentoft continued ...

"There is consequently a need to first illuminate how considerable overlaps in educational intentions and assumptions exist in interdisciplinary learning and PBL, respectively. These overlaps indicate that a problem-based pedagogy could be a potentially attractive strategy when considering curriculum and structure in interdisciplinary education. There is also a need to challenge this observation of overlap by suggesting that a problem-based pedagogy is not by default scaffolding and supporting interdisciplinary learning, but may offer such possibilities only insofar as challenges specifically pertaining to interdisciplinary learning are addressed."

And the conclusion we draw from studying the paper Stentoft, (2017), is: Problem-based learning is not overemphasised as a result of a primary focus on interdisciplinary teams as a way of enacting interdisciplinary graduate practice!

What The Integration Report did not say ...

The Integration Report claims that Zhang and Shen (2015) state that criticisms of this approach have questioned the use of work on interdisciplinary teams as the primary means for enacting interdisciplinary graduate practice: specifically, authors have cautioned that this emphasis may ... neglect the nuances associated with how individuals solve interdisciplinary problems within interdisciplinary teams.

What did Zhang and Shen (2015) actually say? This:

"In this study we investigated how individuals [not teams] solve interdisciplinary problems. Interdisciplinary has various connotations. In this paper, it refers to the connections of different scientific disciplinary fields commonly taught in secondary and college levels, including physics, biology and chemistry.

"We asked the [16] participants to [individually] solve two interdisciplinary science problems on the topic of osmosis.

"Successful interdisciplinary science education needs ...

What *The Integration Report* did not say ...

Zhang and Shen (2015) continued ...

"*Successful interdisciplinary science education needs effective assessments to pinpoint students' difficulties and reflect their actual interdisciplinary reasoning ability. The problem conceptualisation and solving strategies revealed by this study may give directions to interdisciplinary assessment development. [...] conceptualising interdisciplinary problems in a disciplinary way [...] deliberately ignoring one disciplinary factor [...] Assessment items that are designed to elicit these nuanced responses with respect to interdisciplinary reasoning will provide instructors with more information [...].*"

"*This exploratory study had many limitations. [...] we focused on individuals in the study. As collaboration is a common approach in interdisciplinary work, more research is needed to probe into students' collaborative problem-solving from an interdisciplinary perspective.*"

And the conclusion we draw from studying the paper Zhang and Shen (2015) is: It is in fact not the case that the nuances associated with how individuals solve interdisciplinary problems within interdisciplinary teams, are neglected because of a focus on interdisciplinary teams!

What The Integration Report did not say ...

So, in other words we have discovered that ...

- *Disciplines and their knowledge are not necessarily cumulative or complementary. That they are, is an assumption on the part of those that advocate integration, regardless of the emphasis - or lack of it - on interdisciplinary teams as the primary means of enacting interdisciplinary graduate practice.*

- *Problem-based learning is an active learning pedagogical practice that does not automatically provide a framework for interdisciplinary learning, regardless of the emphasis - or lack of it - on interdisciplinary teams as the primary means of enacting interdisciplinary graduate practice.*

- *The nuances associated with how individuals solve interdisciplinary problems within interdisciplinary teams are not neglected because of an emphasis - or lack of it - on interdisciplinary teams as the primary means of enacting interdisciplinary graduate practice.*

Put another way, integration is not what it is all about - interdisciplinarity that is. Which we told you already! So what are the implications of this for The Integration Report with its emphasis on - integration? Better not to engage in critical thinking because when we do, worlds - socially constructed realities - start falling apart.

Disciplinary knowledge cannot be described as branches on the same tree. Well they can of course, but only by those with conservative backward looking world views.

And The Integration Report Says ...

The Integration Report claims that despite the call for
more integrated graduate practices that promote
interdisciplinary work, and despite the existence of
long-standing integrative graduate programs in
established interdisciplinary fields, such approaches
to graduate education are represented in the
literature, for the most part, across and between
similar disciplines. The research literature suggests
that scholars and researchers within the STEM
fields, even those engaging in interdisciplinary work
tend to work with other scholars in these fields.

And the evidence for this is ...

Oh dear! None is presented! Why we wonder?

What do you believe is the case? You can answer
according to your vested interests or you can check.
We checked and found the statement to be ......
You can insert in the blank space anything you
want for we leave the choice of words to you as an
act of participation.

And The Integration Report Says ...

The Integration Report also claims, through reference to a paper by Bullough (2006) that a similar within-disciplinary pattern is observed for educators in the humanities and the humanistic social sciences because these scholars tend to collaborate with peers in other humanities and social science fields, respectively.

And the evidence presented for this is, only the paper by Bullough (2006).

The statement also contradicts that made by Borrego and Newswander (2010), who we quoted out of context for the purpose of rhetoric: "[...] humanities emphasised (solitary) intellectual skills, whereas science and engineering emphasised interpersonal skills [...]."

And The Integration Report Says ...

What does the paper by Bullough (2006) actually say? This in short: The paper is primarily directed at educational researchers engaging in educational research. It argues for the value of humanities to educational research, while noting that the humanities have in the university a poor (self-inflicted) status. Educational researchers we are told need humanities because:

– "Interdisciplinarity [...] when understood in these narrow terms – as bounded by certain sciences and social sciences and the assumptions they share about the nature and purpose of inquiry – is unlikely to get far outside established research biases, habits of mind, and social commitments."

As for the claim about a similar within-disciplinary pattern being observed ... Seek and thou shalt not find!

And The Integration Report Says ...

The Integration Report also asks if the interdisciplinary efforts in graduate education examined in the research literature are effectively interdisciplinary? Are they effective at helping students integrate ideas across disciplines?

Can you see the difficulty with this? The part that asks the question: Are the interdisciplinary efforts in graduate education examined in the research literature effectively interdisciplinary? You will be able to see the problem immediately if you have experience of, or knowledge of the literature on, interdisciplinarity, some of which is actually quoted and referenced in The Integration Report.

The problem is this: often interdisciplinarity is not specifically specified to be ... Its meaning is left open, and can include multidisciplinarity for example. Some of the references we have quoted that relate to interdisciplinary efforts in graduate education do not attempt to pin down the concept. Thus it is not possible to ask, as The Integration Report does, whether interdisciplinary efforts in graduate education examined in the research literature are effectively interdisciplinary. This question though has a purpose — it is part of the Deficit Discourse. Only the reader with the right knowledge will be able to resist the Deficit Discourse. Others will just accept it.

And *The Integration Report* Says ...

The Integration Report also claims that a 2010 literature review of 245 articles about the medical humanities found that 224 of the articles praised the interventions or described and evaluated coursework (Ousager and Johannessen, 2010). While the 224 articles advocated for the inclusion of humanities coursework in medical education, only 9 of the articles sought to study the long-term impacts of medical humanities coursework. These articles examined the outcomes of integrating humanities in undergraduate medical education. One of the 9 papers referenced in the Ousager and Johannessen paper studied two groups of Harvard graduates, one from a traditional medical curriculum and one from a curriculum that was humanities oriented. The literature review conducted by Ousager and Johannessen reveals that, while there is a wealth of course descriptions and advocacy of the medical humanities, there continues to be a shortage of studies reporting evidence.

So what did the literature review actually say? This ...

What The Integration Report did not say ...

The analysis of the 245 articles involved assigning tags to
the papers, from four categories: (1) type of publication;
(2) sector of the major humanities field treated; (3)
suggested benefits; (4) general tone. The papers were
also classified into four types: (1) pleading the case; (2)
course descriptions and evaluations; (3) seeking evidence
of long-term impacts; (4) holding the horses.

68 of the 245 articles were categorised as pleading the
case, 146 as course descriptions and evaluations, 9 as
seeking evidence of long-term impact, 10 as holding the
horses. 224 articles either praised the (potential) effects
of humanities on medical education, or described
existing or planned courses, without offering substantial
evidence of any long-term impact of these curricular
activities.

Somewhat similar in fact to what has been noted about
other artist interventions in organisations – yes it is the
case that these interventions in medical education often
involve artists! One might ask therefore – why all these
anecdotal tales by, or about, artists?

The answer has something to do with the image of the
artist is western societies – the legend, myth and magic
associated with the artist in these societies. It is a
cultural thing – back to the Leonardo mythology!

And *The Integration Report* Says ...

The Integration Report will enthusiastically tell you
  about *Fusion Theory*. No, not the fusion of atoms,
  but the fusion of arts and humanities with STEM.
  In particular, the so-called Brighton Fuse Report –
  which is another art/humanities advocacy report.

Brighton – A Tale of Two Cities! Literally! An up-area
  – called Hove – and the rest, called Brighton. And
  for all the fusing that is going on, you will still find
  people begging on the streets! Begging on the streets
  of Brighton! But hey, that's enough of reality –
  time for some fantasy, the fantasy of fusion!

The Integration Report tells the story of Brighton,
  which is akin to Silicon Valley in California.
  Apparently!

So what is it that *The Integration Report* is not telling.
  There must of something. Of course there is! This
  ...

What The Integration Report did not say ...

The *Brighton Fuse Report* will not tell you which particular humanities subjects have been fused with STEM, which would be useful to know! So if you are wondering why humanities graduates in history, comparative religion, philosophy, linguistics, law, and so forth, make for a good fusion with STEM people, then you will be disappointed for answers to such questions are not to be found. You will in fact notice the absence of case study material that might have provided some useful insights and understanding of what and why.

The *Integration Report* did not mention (no-one ever does!) this comment concerning barriers to growth: "One puzzling result was a perception of the artistic community as a barrier by some business owners. In some cases this was substantial: 15% of marketing services firms, and 21% of firms with more than 25 employees had this negative view of the local artistic community. The qualitative research leads us to believe that this view is rooted in a suspicion of the 'bohemian' lifestyle of artists and creative people. Many of the Managing Directors of firms referred to a mix of creativity, lifestyle and a desire for an 'easy life' rather than a hard work ethic. This is seen as the downside of Brighton's creativity and seaside quality of life."

Perhaps it's those people begging on the streets?

And The Integration Report Says ...

The Integration Report also mentions something called the Connections Program, which it is claimed was developed in response to calls for engineering education reform in the mid-1990s, and was designed to help students form connections in their first-year courses and understand the importance of their first-year studies by allowing them to develop appropriate and significant links among disciplines. The relevant reference is Olds and Miller (2004, p. 25). Students who participated in the program enrolled in science and engineering courses where faculty used integrated project modules and active-learning strategies, participated in a two-semester interdisciplinary seminar that further developed and explored the interconnectedness of appropriate topics from each of the first-year science, humanities, and engineering courses (p. 25), and engaged in peer study group systems ...

And The Integration Report Says ...

The Integration Report claims that Olds and Miller (2004) found that average engineering students who participated in the Connections Program graduated at rates approximately 25 percent higher than students in the traditional curriculum. Additionally, it is stated, through a follow-up survey 5 years later, these students indicated that their experience in Connections enhanced their academic preparation by helping them make connections among course topics, improving their critical thinking abilities, setting a context for their science and engineering studies, increasing their awareness of ethical issues, and strengthening their communication skills. Furthermore, it is claimed, Olds and Miller noted that resources spent to have top faculty teach and mentor first-year students resulted in increased retention and overall satisfaction with the educational experience.

So what did Olds and Miller (2004) actually say? This ...

What The Integration Report did not say …

"The *Connections Programme*, which was only applied in first-year studies, modified existing pedagogical practices (primarily passive lectures in most courses) to include extensive use of active-learning and cooperative learning strategies, team teaching, and writing as a learning and inquiry tool, and, developed a peer study group system to encourage interpersonal growth and support among *Connections* students.

"Particularly in the second pilot course where the seminar was redesigned to emphasize the role of faculty and peer mentoring and learning community development, students believed that social connections were more meaningful to them than the topical connections originally envisioned by the *Connections* faculty and as exemplified by the original learning objectives of the program."

What The Integration Report did not say ...

And ...

"Based on our analysis of the survey, we believe that a significant reason for the greater persistence rate of the Connections students was the learning community that they and the Connections faculty formed, especially in the second year of the program. Tinto [1] enumerates four outcomes associated with learning communities he studied, all of which were borne out in our study."

Those four outcomes are:

— *Students in learning communities tend to form self-supporting groups;*

— *Learning community students become more actively involved in classroom learning;*

— *Participation in a learning community seems to enhance the quality of student learning;*

— *Learning community students persist at a higher rate than comparative students in traditional curriculum.*

What The Integration Report did not say ...

As a result, Olds and Millar (2004) drew the
   following conclusions:

Mentoring makes a difference – interactions with
   faculty and peers was the single most positive
   aspect of the students' experiences.

Learning communities are important – students who
   feel they belong from the beginning are more
   likely to persist.

Content of integrated programmes, while important,
   does not have the impact that personal contact
   does.

Resources spent up front to allow top faculty to teach
   and mentor first-year students pays dividends in
   increased retention.

And The Integration Report Says ...

The Integration Report makes the claim that courses that integrate the arts, humanities, and STEMM fields are also associated with increased student motivation and engagement. They state that Olin College of Engineering offered two options to students taking an introductory materials science course: an integrated materials science-history course co-taught by faculty in engineering and history, or a non-integrated course taught only by an engineering professor. Although both courses were project based and had similar structures, students who participated in the integrated course demonstrated increased motivation and engagement in self-regulated learning strategies over the term compared with students in the non-integrated course, as measured by the Situational Motivation Scale and the Motivated Strategies for Learning Questionnaire. Additionally, students in the integrated course self-reported using critical thinking skills in their work more frequently and had higher self-efficacy and valuing of learning tasks than students in the non-integrated course.

The relevant reference is Stolk and Martello (2015).

What The Integration Report did not say ...

As Stolk and Martello (2015) is actually the one and only clear (and believable) case of the integration of a humanities course into a STEMM course, we will look even closer at this one.

Stolk and Martello (2015) present an analysis of two material sciences courses – one integrated, and the other (termed as) non-integrated. As integration though is not defined by *The Integration Report*, it is not clear if the non-integrated course does in fact really exclude integration!

In the conclusions of the paper, Stolk and Martello *sing the praises* of integrated courses. "The findings in this study indicate that disciplinary integration offers significant benefits to student motivation and self-directed learning skills. Compared to a non-integrated project-based materials science course, students in an integrated materials science-history of technology course showed higher ... "

But if you were to examine the paper – critically examine it in the style of the much vaunted critical thinking – you will discover that it is not the case that "The findings in this study indicate that disciplinary integration offers significant benefits to student motivation ... "

What The Integration Report did not say ...

Most of the statistical models in Stolk and Martello's 2015
   paper have no statistical significance. Moreover, both
   courses – the integrated one and the non-integrated
   one – deploy active learning pedagogies.

The few models that do have statistical significance,
   present results that are probably of little (or no?)
   practical significance! What do we mean? Wait for a
   moment ...

As regards student motivation and student engagement in
   cognitive, behaviour and contextual self-regulation, in
   both cases there is statistical significance in the
   models comparing the integrated and non-integrated
   courses (Tables 3 and 4 in the paper).

What do Stolk and Martello have to say about student
   motivation and student engagement in cognitive,
   behaviour and contextual self-regulation, when
   comparing the two courses?

What The Integration Report did not say ...

About motivation the authors state: "Small yet statistically significant differences between the integrated and non-integrated courses are apparent on the SIMS subscales, as well as on the MSLQ task value measure. The relatively small differences in student motivation between the integrated and non-integrated courses are likely due to the shared design features across these two project-based environments. Both courses are based on pedagogically sound methods of supporting positive motivations. [...] students in both the integrated and non-integrated project based courses have substantial choice and control (autonomy) over their learning topics and processes. In addition, students in both courses are able to identify the practical relevance of their work, as they examine materials in the context of product design, manufacturing, use, and disposal."

What The Integration Report did not say ...

They then go on to say: *"Our findings may indicate that applications centred project work alone can provide high enough levels of autonomy, competence, and relatedness to promote intrinsic motivation. The between-groups analysis of the course-level task value measure and the activity-level SIMS data suggest, however, that engineering students do realize increased personal interest and value in considering technology in context. "*

As regards student engagement in cognitive, behaviour and contextual self-regulation, the authors state: *"Between-groups analysis of the post-test subscale means (Fig. 2) revealed higher use of critical thinking skills at post-test in the integrated course compared to the non-integrated course (Table 3). This indicates that the integrated projects prompted more use of strategies that involve applying previous knowledge to new situations, making decisions, playing with ideas and developing new concepts, critically evaluating evidence, assertions, and conclusions. "*

What The Integration Report did not say ...

What the authors do not tell the reader are the effect sizes. We computed these using the data provided in the paper (Tables 3 and 4). The effect sizes (Cohen's d) lie between 0.4 and 0.1 (approx.). Specifically: approx 0.4 for Table 3 results and approx 0.1 for Table 4 results. Hedge's g effect size gives the same result.

What does the above mean?

The meaning is this: most effect sizes are less than small, with two lying between small and medium, which is the reason why we said that the results are probably of little (or no) practical significance — put another way, they are probably not worth the effort.

One has to ask why no effect sizes are given in the paper. If they had been given then the way that the results are presented would have been very different. Less inclined towards motivated reasoning perhaps? This paper well illustrates what we said earlier about statistics and their use and misuse.

What The Integration Report did not say ...

Also raised in our mind, because hypotheses are
   mentioned, is the question of whether this paper is an
   example of hypothesis hacking, or just an example of
   poor method and analysis.

This highlights the issue that is the research integrity
   problem – there is no way of knowing what one is
   dealing with and whether one can take – accept –
   what is stated in a paper.

But what about the gender issues? Indeed what about
   them!

As regards gender issues, the paper notes that: "A
   between-groups, gender-based analysis of the
   significant post-test differences (Table 7 and Fig. 3)
   shows that women in the integrated course report
   higher task value, self-efficacy, and critical thinking
   strategy use compared to women in the non-integrated
   course. Men in the two courses, however, show no
   significant post-test differences on the MSLQ
   subscales. In short, the gender-based analyses support
   our hypothesis regarding the benefits that
   contextualization through integrated course approaches
   can provide to women in engineering."

What The Integration Report did not say ...

Looks good! But what about the effect sizes? We calculated these. We found for Table 7 that effect sizes (again Cohen's d) were around 0.6 (approx.). In other words effect sizes were medium. But before you rush off and implement an integrated course, there are a few provisos to take note of:

We are dealing here with a first year introductory materials science course, with students that already had experience of project-based pedagogies that enable them to shape their work around personal interests and goals, in the specific context of a small private college.

The authors also note that: "The MSLQ survey was designed with more conventional college classrooms in mind, it may be that some of the MSLQ survey prompts are difficult for students to interpret in the context of project-based activities."

They raise this point as a possible explanation for the lack of statistical significance in many of their statistical models, but it could also work the other way — it could also explain why there is statistical significance, when perhaps there should be none!

What *The Integration Report* did not say ...

And last, but not least – the sample sizes are also too
small to draw any conclusions. When sample sizes
are increased and different contexts become
encapsulated in the statistical models, then it is very
possible that these effects might just simply vanish
into thin air. Or to paraphrase Shakespeare's
Prospero: "These effects, as I foretold you, were all
spirits, and are melted into air, into thin air."

Time to recap about statistical methods ...

For the Understanding of that which STARTS to
STEAM, to the Statisticians Turn – 7

Quoting from Greenland, et al (2016):

"All statistical methods (whether frequentist or Bayesian,
or for testing or estimation, or for inference or
decision) make extensive assumptions about the
sequence of events that led to the results presented—
not only in the data generation, but in the analysis
choices. Thus, to allow critical evaluation, research
reports (including meta-analyses) should describe in
detail the full sequence of events that led to the
statistics presented, including the motivation for the
study, its design, the original analysis plan, the
criteria used to include and exclude subjects (or
studies) and data, and a thorough description of all
the analyses that were conducted."

We will now examine a case where the above is violated.
The case of Art Fosters Scientific Success ...

Unexpected Item in Bagging Area – Religion Fosters Scientific Success

How many priests or monks can you name that have made contributions to the world of science, technology, engineering or mathematics? If you look you will find that there are many. In fact if you were to make a list it would be longer than any list of artists, unless of course you dwell in the art-science lovers socially constructed reality, and are intent on maintaining your beliefs in spite of empirical evidence to the contrary.

Here are a few names, others you can find using Google:

- Roger Bacon (c1219-c1292): A thirteenth century English Franciscan friar who is credited with making pioneering steps towards the development of experimental method, as well as making early contributions to optics and astronomy.

- John Peckham (c1230-1292): Archbishop of Canterbury from 1279 to 1292, produced works on optics and astronomy and is believed to have been influenced by Bacon's views on the value of experimental science.

- William of Ockham (1285-1347): An English Franciscan friar who devised the methodological principle known as Ockham's Razor, and produced works on physics and logic.

- Nicholas of Cusa (1401-1464): A fifteenth-century cardinal in the Church of Rome who produced mathematical and astronomical treatises, and is credited as being an advocate of the idea that the earth is not at rest and is not the centre of the universe.

- Leon Battista Alberti (1404-1472): A fifteenth-century priest who practiced as an architect and who used Euclidean geometry and optics to provide artists with the means of calculating linear point perspective.

- Nicholas Copernicas (1473-1543): Held ecclesiastic office as Canon of Frombork Cathedral (now in Poland), and developed a heliocentric (though still incorrect) model of the solar system.

- Isaac Newton (1643-1727): A mathematician, as well as an alchemist and amateur theologian, whose significant contribution to mathematics and science are so well known as not to need mentioning.

- Emanual Swedenborg (1688-1772): A Swedish theologian who believed that he was divinely inspired and who undertook many studies of anatomy and physiology and is credited as anticipating the neuron concept.

- Thomas Bayes (c1701-1761): An English Presbyterian minister, who formulated what is now called Bayes Theorem.

- Gilbert White (1720-1793): An English parson and pioneering naturalist who is best known for his book *The Natural History and Antiquities of Selborne*.

- Thomas Robert Malthus (1766-1834): An English cleric who contributed to demography, most notably through his controversial book *An Essay on the Principle of Population*.

- William Whewell (1794-1866): An English Anglican priest who contributed to the philosophy of science, notably through the study of the history of science, producing a two-volume book with the title *The Philosophy of the Inductive Sciences, Founded upon their History*, in which he presents consilience as one of a number of aphorism of the inductive sciences.

- Francis Orpen Morris (1810-1893): An Irish clergyman and ornithologist who wrote several books cataloguing British birds.

- Gregor Mendle (1822-1884): An Austrian Augustinian friar who made pioneering contributions to plant genetics, most notably, the rules of heredity known as Mendelian inheritance.

- Georges Lemaître (1894-1966): A Belgian catholic priest who held the post of professor of physics at the Catholic University of Louvain. He was the first person to identify that the recession of nearby galaxies can be explained by a theory of an expanding universe and formulated what is now called the Hubble–Lemaître law, making the first estimate of the Hubble constant in 1927.

- And many more …

Art-science lovers believe (although they may not realise it) that artists, being special people, have special access to reality. Why then does religion foster scientific success? Is it because priests and monks, being able to see into the mind of God, have special access to reality? Or is it the case that those listed (and the many others) being educated people, able to read and write in Latin, with access to libraries (with their Latin versions of Greek and Arabic texts), with the free time and the motivation, were in fact the main people able to make contributions to science? Until that is, their role started to be taken over by well-off Gentleman natural philosophers, which ultimately led to the emergence of professional salaried scientists.

And The Integration Report Says ...

The Integration Report mentions a 2008 study undertaken by Bernstein and others who, it is claimed, found that very accomplished scientists, including Nobel Laureates, National Academy of Sciences members, and Royal Society members, were significantly more likely to engage in arts and crafts and identify as artists than average scientists and the general public. The study is reported in Root-Bernstein et al., (2008). Compared with scientists who are members of Sigma Xi, a society in which, it is claimed, any working scientist can be a member, Nobel Laureates were 2 times as likely to be photographers, 4 times as likely to be musicians, 17 times as likely to be artists, 15 times as likely to be crafts people, 25 times as likely to be creative writers, and 22 times as likely to be performers.

We will now start to show you why this is just plain nonsense and in doing so demonstrate why you can no longer believe what people in authority say, especially researchers (with and without artists in residence!) ...

What The Integration Report did not say ...

The title of the paper is: Arts Fosters Scientific Success: Avocations of Nobel, National Academy, Royal Society, and Sigma Xi Members.

The problems with this paper are so extensive that one could write a book about them – a book that would position the paper as, at best, a piece of poor quality research, and at worst, a case study that illustrates the nature of the research integrity crisis, with the content of the paper being just a piece of ideological nonsense dressed-up as the results of sound research.

The problems with the paper start with the title – the work in the paper has nothing to do with the claim announced by the title – Art Fosters Scientific Success, nor the claim that it is addressing the avocations of a number of groups of scientists.

Unexpected Item in Bagging Area – Apocryphal

Apocryphal

Apocryphal

Apocryphal

Apocryphal

Apocryphal

Apocryphal

Apocryphal

Apocryphal

Apocryphal

Apocryphal

Apocryphal

Apocryphal

Apocryphal

Apocryphal

(of a story) of doubtful authenticity, although widely circulated as being true.

What The Integration Report did not say ...

As soon as one encounters the content, one hits problems. You will not find any explanation for example, how hobbies were differentiated from avocations, nor any explanation why the term avocation is used rather than hobby. Lack of transparency about assumptions?

The latter is important, not least for the reason that some of the data, possibly most, relates to hobbies. The Sigma Xi data is the clearest example of this. Lack of transparency about assumptions?

The paper has several errors and dubious statements. One of these is actually reproduced in The Integration Report. In the paper it is claimed that "[...] members of Sigma Xi, a society in which any working scientist can be a member [...]". This is incorrect. To become a member one has to be nominated by two people and one must meet the membership criteria. Also the membership includes engineers (Sigma Xi was actually founded by engineers) as well as scientists. Lack of transparency about assumptions?

What The Integration Report did not say ...

Another incorrect statement concerns the 1982 US Survey of Public Participation in the Arts, where the paper states that, "[...] no crafts data was collected [...]". But the 1982 survey did collect crafts data. Two questions relating to crafts were included in the survey. The following questions are taken from the Codebook for 1982 Data:

- *During the last 12 months, did you work with pottery, ceramics, jewellery, or do any leatherwork, metalwork, or similar?*

- *During the last 12 months, did you do any weaving, crocheting, quilting, needlepoint, sewing, or similar crafts?*

Perhaps a small point (yet one that illustrates the sloppiness in the paper) is that the paper refers to Members of the Royal Society. The Royal Society does not have any members! It has Fellows — scientists, mathematicians and engineers — who are elected by other fellows on the basis of a person's outstanding contribution to science, mathematics or engineering. We mention this point for a reason ...

What The Integration Report did not say ...

And that reason is, Table 2 in the paper provides a list
of Scientists Who Publicly Exhibited and/or Sold
Visual Art or Sculpture, Published Works of Fiction,
or Publicly Performed Musical Pieces. The most
obvious – glaring – error in this table is the
inclusion of CP Snow, who is designated as RS, that
is to say a member (Fellow) of the Royal Society. CP
Snow was never elected a Fellow of the Royal
Society, for the reasons we have already explained –
he was a not a successful scientist.

Snow is not the only error. Another is Conrad
Waddington. He was a Fellow of the Royal Society
but there is no evidence, not in the reference
material quoted in the paper, nor in other documents,
that he ever exhibited or sold visual art, nor for that
matter, ever painted!

The table also includes the name of the theoretical
physicist Richard Feynman, who is designated is the
table as NL – a Nobel Laureate. Feynman did paint,
but this he took up later in his life, two years in fact,
before he won a Nobel Prize. And there is, obviously
no connection at all between the two events!

What The Integration Report did not say ...

The last point – temporal issues – is a matter that is ignored in the paper. There are many more. Particularly there is the question of whether any of these so called polymaths, were any good at their hobby, good enough to be a professional rather than just, for example, a Sunday painter? Moreover, the paper also ignores the matter of socialisation into the arts at an early stage and socio-economics – because both are relevant to the matter of adoption of art and crafts hobbies.

The above errors also have implications for the quality of the work. Self-evidently! What value is the data that has been created?

Thus we ask: are the results obtained really an observable effect, or are the results a consequence of the epistemological and ontological incompatibilities among the data used? One day, in a future work, we will provide an answer to this question. For the moment we leave you with two remarks ...

234

And the First – Near, Far, Wherever you are ...

If art does, in some way, foster scientific success, or
provide useful skills, then there must be a theoretical
explanation for this in psychology. There is!

The theory has a name – it is called *Far Transfer*. The
only problem is that there is no convincing evidence
that it happens. It is in fact highly controversial.

A paper published in the Psychology Journal, *Current
Directions in Psychological Science* in 2017, concluded,
based on a meta analysis across three areas, that far
transfer learning rarely occurs. Particularly, the work
showed that effect sizes are inversely proportional to
quality of the experimental design. In other words
high quality experimental designs do not find *Far
Transfer* effects.

The three areas considered in the research were: the
effects of playing chess and of taking music
instruction on children's cognitive development and
academic skills, and the effect of working memory
training on the same two variables. In other words, in
the case of music training, there is no such thing as
the Mozart Effect!

The message is clear – if you want to train for a skill, do
it directly, which is the *Near Transfer* theory.

And the Second – on the matter of Research Integrity ...

"Fraud is very likely second to incompetence in generating erroneous results, though it is hard to tell for certain."

The Economist, 2013

"The enquiry could not be blind to evident violations of the basic rules of sound scientific research. The enquiry committees were forced increasingly to the conclusion that, even in the absence of fraud in the strict sense, there was a general culture of careless, selective and uncritical handling of research and data. The observed flaws were not minor normal imperfections in statistical processing, or experimental design and execution, but violations of fundamental rules of proper scientific research with a possibly severe impact on the research conclusions. The enquiry committees are of the opinion that this culture partly explains why the fraud was not detected earlier."

Flawed Science: The Fraudulent Research Practices of Social Psychologist Diederik Stapel, 2012

Unexpected Item in Bagging Area – Creative People and their Love of Dictators and their Totalitarian and Authoritarian Regimes

How many people from the world of the arts and media (writers, authors, actors, directors, journalists and others), displayed an astonishing lack of judgement, of critical thinking, by becoming apologists (to varying degrees) for, and sometimes supporters of, dictators and the social-political systems that they created? We are talking about individuals, for example, who had, at a minimum, positive things to say about Mussolini and his Italian Fascists, Hitler and his National Socialists, and Stalin and his Soviet Communists. Sometimes these people from the world of arts and media left the world of reality far behind and said the most extraordinary things about these dictators and their regimes! We will just focus on these figures from the 1930s, and leave aside those who have done the same in more recent times for other dictators such as Mao, Castro, Pol Pot, Hugo Chavez, Omar Torrijos, Bashir al-Assad, Kim Il Sung, and Saddam Hussein.

Here are some names:

- Walter Duranty: An American journalist, apologist for Stalin, defender of Soviet brutality and dictatorship, and uncritical believer in the truth of Soviet propaganda.

- Wyndham Lewis: An English writer and painter, known for his early support (eventually revised) of Hitler as a man of peace!

- Knut Hamsun: A Norwegian writer, winner of the 1920 Nobel Prize for literature, and Nazi supporter and collaborator and an apologist for Hitler.

- Ezra Pound: An American modernist poet noted for his anti-Semitism and his support for Mussolini and Hitler. Pound collaborated with the Italian Fascist regime during the Second World War and was arrested in 1945 by the American Army on charges of Treason.

- Romain Rolland: A French dramatist and novelist, winner of the Nobel Prize for literature and a leading supporter of Stalin who he is reported to have described as being the greatest man of his time.

- George Bernard Shaw: The famous Irish playwright also known for his belief in dictatorship as the only viable form of government and his admiration of Mussolini and Stalin, as well as the favourable comments he made about Hitler, he was an uncritical champion in the 1930s of Stalin and his regime.

- H.G. Wells: The well known English writer and novelist is less well known as someone drawn to both Italian Fascism and Soviet Communism with positive things to say about both, although he was willing to be critical about some aspects of these regimes.

- Henry Williamson: An English author, member of the British Union of Fascists, who believed that Hitler was a good man!

- W.B. Yeats: An Irish poet attributed as being anti-Semitic and a supporter of Fascism. Yeats has the distinction of being mentioned by CP Snow in his 1959 Rede Lecture (*The Two Cultures*) as being an example (along with Pound and Lewis) of a politically wicked literary intellectual from the 1930s whose views helped to bring Auschwitz that much closer.

In case you do not know ...

Two Nouns Unalike in Meaning

From the Online Oxford English Dictionary:

— *Misinformation: False or inaccurate information, especially that which is deliberately intended to deceive.*

— *Disinformation: False information which is intended to mislead, especially propaganda issued by a government organization to a rival power or the media.*

Note the difference!

A Declaration of Interest ...

Yes, we have an interest that we will now announce.

Our interest is in flawed decision making, especially on the part of people one might expect to be able to take sound decisions, based on that which is relevant, including sound evidence. People such as those from the world of STEM for example, or those who work in technocratic organisations such as the European Commission.

That which STARTS to STEAM – both examples of a massively flawed decision making ...

What is interesting is that those from the world of STEM are the ones most inclined to believe that which STARTS to STEAM!

New Leonardos in ignorance dwelling ...

Colliding Worlds – Socially Constructed Realities in Conflict

There are those who are part of one socially constructed reality (Enlightenment Fundamentalists, Believers in Scientism, Technocrats, ...) proclaiming the coming age of the rule of science and reason, attacking anyone (from other socially constructed realities) who dare to criticise science or technology, while as they do so, creating their own sacred (secular theological) texts (often based on narrow perceptions, misunderstandings, ideology – a scientific reduction to ignorance), while also appropriating art so that, like past totalitarians, they can achieve a spiritual union with the masses, engineer their souls (Stalin's phrase), and induce changes in their individual and collective behaviour (the European Commission's phrase).

Wanting a share of money and power, artists (and others) are busy creating their own socially constructed reality, but this time centred around the ideology of liberal arts – the people who believe that are able to think – so that they can loyally serve, without thinking, the coming new world order of science and reason!

241

Colliding Worlds – Socially Constructed Realities in Conflict

We think that the world is in serious trouble because the free people do not, in actual fact, think in the way they believe, while the few who do try to think –slowly – are ignored! As was the case with National Socialism – not only were those who warned ignored, they were also dismissed as being out-dated and were often vilified as well.

Every new generation does indeed find new ways of making the same old mistakes ...

What you do not know that you do not know

The Emperor is wearing no clothes,

but they will not listen.

Ears are turned inwards,

hearing only the mind's

own soothing words.

Eyes too only see,

the beautiful vision of

what the mind allows to be seen.

So then do they blindly stumble,

onward to the edge of doom.

The End

And this is what you do not know you do not know ...

244

"The ideal subject of totalitarian rule is not the convinced Nazi or the convinced Communist, but people for whom the distinction between fact and fiction (i.e., the reality of experience) and the distinction between true and false (i.e., the standards of thought) no longer exist."

Hannah Arendt, 1951
The Origins of Totalitarianism

Beauty can save the world!

Unexpected Item in Bagging Area – Illusory Truth

Illusory Truth – what psychologists call the *Illusory Truth Effect* – is an observed phenomenon where people come to believe falsehoods because these have so often been repeated, that they can be recalled with ease and this fluency of recall has become a cue to infer validity. We have encountered illusory truths in this work, for example, the things that people believe about Leonardo da Vinci, which do not though, stand-up to close scrutiny!

Here is a modern illusory truth: The German supermarket chains ALDI and Lidl are each owned by two different people who are brothers. In other words, one brother owns ALDI and the other owns Lidl. This came about because of a disagreement between the two brothers. The part (about the ownership) is not true, and the other part is also false in the context of ALDI and Lidl, but you will find people who believe the statement about ALDI and Lidl is true because it is often repeated (on social networks?). If you fact check the statement you will discover that there are two independent companies carrying the name ALDI – ALDI Nord and ALDI Süd, neither of which have any connection with Lidl, which is owned by a different family. The split of ALDI into two independent companies happened as a result of a disagreement between the two brothers running the family business. So each brother ended up owning their own ALDI. Or is this an illusory truth too?

The results of a research study, published in 2020, into the *Illusory Truth Effect*, shows that the *Illusory Truth Effect* is invariant across personality types – it happens to people regardless of their cognitive ability (intelligence), their need for cognitive closure (tolerance or intolerance of ambiguity), and their cognitive style (intuitive versus analytic thinking).

Thus do the social sciences aid understanding of … why so many people from the world of STEM and their artists in residence believe so much that is plain nonsense. Other understandings can be found, as we have demonstrated.

There is no single reality invariant across individuals, nations and cultures – and disciplines too. Be careful what you believe!

And that is a totally *True* story

The End

Bibliography

Aleksandr Solzhenitsyn Center (n.d.). *Autobiography*. Retrieved from: https://www.solzhenitsyncenter.org/autobiography/

Anderson, H.C. (2008). *The Emperor's New Clothes (M.R. James, Trans.)*. Retrieved from https://www.gutenberg.ca/ebooks/andersen-emperor/andersen-emperor-00-h.html. (*Originally published in 1837*).

Anonymous (2008*). Jumping Through Hoops. Why do we continue to lie on funding applications and evaluation reports?* Retrieved from http://ixia-info.com/new-writing/jumpingthroughhoops/#4.1

Apple Computers (24 October 2019). *Apple Leadership: Jonathon Ive – Chief Design Officer*. Retrieved from: https://www.apple.com/uk/leadership/jonathan-ive/

Arendt, H. (2017). *The Origins of Totalitarianism*. London: Penguin Classics. (*Originally published in 1951*).

Aristotle (1922). *De Caelo (J. L. Stocks, Trans.)*. London: Clarendon Press.

Ashby, E. (1958). *Technology and the Academics: An Essay on Universities and the Scientific Revolution*. London: MacMillan & Co.

Barrowclough, D. (2016). *Digging for Hitler: The Nazi Archaeologists Search for an Aryan Past*. Stroud: Fonthill Media.

BBC News (9 July 2018). *Nissan Admits Falsifying Emission Tests in Japan*. Retrieved from https://www.bbc.co.uk/news/business-44763905

BBC News (11 April 2019). *Brexit: All you need to know about the UK leaving the EU*. Retrieved from: https://www.bbc.co.uk/news/uk-politics-32810887

BBC TV (23 November 1981). *Horizon Programme: The Pleasure of Finding Things Out*.

Berger, J. (1972). *Ways of Seeing*. London: Penguin Books.

Berlin, I. (2013). *The Hedgehog and the Fox: An Essay on Tolstoy's View of History*. London: Weidenfeld & Nicolson (*Originally published in 1953*).

Berthoin Antal, A. (2009*). Transforming Organisations with the Arts: Research Framework for Evaluating the Effects of Artistic Interventions in Organizations*. TILTEUROPE Research Report. Retrieved from https://www.wzb.eu/sites/default/files/u30/researchreport.pdf

Berthoin Antal, A. and Strauβ, A. (2016). Multistakeholder perspectives on searching for evidence of values-added in artistic interventions in organisation. In: U. Johansson Sköldberg, J. Woodilla and A. Berthoin Antal (eds.), *Artistic Interventions in Organizations* (pp. 37-59). Abingdon: Routledge.

Berthoin Antal, A., Woodilla, J. and Johansson Sköldberg, U. (2016). From Revolution to Evolution … and Back Again. In: U. Johansson Sköldberg, J. Woodilla and A. Berthoin Antal (eds.), *Artistic Interventions in Organizations* (pp. 241-249). Abingdon: Routledge.

248

Blake, W. (2001). *The Complete Illuminated Books*. London: Thames & Hudson.

Bopegedera, A. M. R. P. (2005). The Art and Science of Light: An Interdisciplinary Teaching and Learning Experience. *Journal of Chemical Education, 82(1)* pp. 55-59

Borrego, M., and Newswander, L. K. (2010). Definitions of interdisciplinary research: Toward graduate-level interdisciplinary learning outcomes. *Review of Higher Education 34(1)*, pp. 61-84.

Bowden, M.A. (2010). *Creativity and Art*. Oxford: Oxford Univ. Press.

Broertjes, W. (1932). *Method of Maintaining Secrecy in the Transmission of Wireless Telegraphic Messages*. US Patent No. 1,869,659.

Bullough, R. V. (2006). Developing interdisciplinary researchers: What ever happened to the humanities in education? *Educational Researcher 35(8)*, pp. 3-10.

Burke, E. (1910). *Reflections on the Revolution in France*. London: J.M. Dent & Sons (*Originally published in 1790*).

Cave, H. (2017). From STEM to STEAM. *Professional Engineer, 30(10)*, pp. 33-37.

Commons Select Committee on Science and Technology (2017). *Inquiry into Research Integrity: Terms of Reference*. Retrieved from https://www.parliament.uk/business/committees/committees-a-z/commons-select/science-and-technology-committee/news-parliament-2017/research-integrity-tor-17-19/

Commons Select Committee on Science and Technology (2018). *Research Integrity: Sixth Report of Session 2017-19*. Retrieved from https://publications.parliament.uk/pa/cm201719/cmselect/cmsctech/350/350.pdf

Commons Select Committee on Digital, Culture, Media and Sport (2018). *Disinformation and 'fake news': Interim Report*. Fifth Report of Session 2017–19. Retrieved from https://publications.parliament.uk/pa/cm201719/cmselect/cmcumeds/363/363.pdf

Colquhoun, D. (2014). An Investigation of the False Discovery Rate and the Misinterpretation of p-values. *R. Soc. Open sci. 1: 140216*. http://dx.doi.org/10.1098/rsos.140216

Darsø, L. (2004). *Artful Creation: Learning-tales of Arts-in-Business*. Frederiksberg: Sanfundslitteratur.

De Keersmaecker, J., Dunning, D., Pennycook, G., Rand, D. G., Sanchez, C., Unkelbach, C. and Roets, A. (2010). Investigating the robustness of the illusory truth effect across individual differences in cognitive ability, need for cognitive closure, and cognitive style. *Personality and Social Psychology Bulletin 46(2)*, pp.204-215.

Derbyshire J. (2016). *Degrees of Separation*. FT Magazine. Retrieved from: https://www.ft.com/content/3cc5d6b6-da81-11e5-98fd-06d75973fe09

Dostoevsky, F. (1887). *The Idiot (F. Whishaw, Trans.)*. London: Vizetelly & Co.

E&T Magazine Editorial Staff (June 6, 2018). *FCC Found to have Implied False Cyberattack During Net Neutrality Repeal*. Retrieved from https://eandt.theiet.org/content/articles/2018/06/fcc-implied-false-cyberattack-narrative-during-net-neutrality-repeal-emails-show/

European Commission (2017). *Horizon 2020 Work Programme 2018-2020: Information and Communication Technologies*. Retrieved from http://ec.europa.eu/research/participants/data/ref/h2020/wp/2018-2020/main/h2020-wp1820-leit-ict_en.pdf.

European Commission (26 April 2018). *Press Release: Tackling Online Disinformation*. Retrieved from: http://europa.eu/rapid/press-release_MEMO-18-3371_en.htm

European Commission (2018). *A Multi-dimensional Approach to Disinformation - Report of the Independent High level Group on Fake News and Online Disinformation*. Retrieved from https://ec.europa.eu/digital-single-market/en/news/final-report-high-level-expert-group-fake-news-and-online-disinformation

Evans, R. and Marvin, S. (2006). Researching the sustainable city: three modes of interdisciplinarity. *Environment and Planning A, 38*, pp. 1009-1028.

FEAT Project (2016). *FEAT @ Ars Electronica*, Workshop Result Paper, June 8th, Linz, Austria. Retrieved from http://www.featart.eu/fileadmin/user_upload/FEAT_3rdWS_result_paper.pdf.

Feynman R.P. and Leighton, R. (1985). *Surely You're Joking Mr Feynman!: Adventures of a Curious Character as told to Ralph Leighton, (E. Hutchings, Ed.)*. London: W.W. Norton.

Friedman, K. and Ox, J. (2017). Phd in Art and Design. *Leonardo, 50(5)*, pp. 515-519.

Gelb, M. (2004). *How to Think like Leonardo da Vinci: Seven Steps to Genius Everyday*. London: Thorsons.

Gibbons, M., Limoges, C., Nowotny, H., Schwartzman, S., Scott, P. and Trow, M. (1994). *The New Production of Knowledge: The Dynamics of Science and Research in Contemporary Societies*. London: Sage Publication.

Glinkowski, P. and Bamford A. (2009). *Insight and Exchange: An Evaluation of the Wellcome Trust's Sciart Programme*. London: Wellcome Trust. Retrieved from https://wellcome.ac.uk/sites/default/files/wtx057228_0.pdf

Glover, A. (2013). *The Role of Science in Future EU Policy Making*. First Spinoza Lecture, November, European Academy of Sciences and the Arts. Retrieved from http://www.euro-acad.eu/downloads/events/Glover_Lecture_Agenda_19_Nov_2013.pdf

Golman, R., Hagmann, D. and Loewenstein, G. (2017). Information Avoidance. *J. of Economic Literature*, 55(1), pp. 96-135.

Golomstock, I. (2011). *Totalitarian Art: In the Soviet Union, the Third Reich, Fascist Italy and the People's Republic of China (R. Chandler, Trans.)*. London: Duckworth.

Greenland, S., Senn, S.J., Rothman, K.J., Carlin, J.B., Poole,C., Goodman, S.N. and Altman, D.G. (2016). Statistical Tests, P-values, Confidence Intervals, and Power: A Guide to Misinterpretations. *Eur J Epidemiol, 31*, pp 337–350
DOI 10.1007/s10654-016-0149-3

Hawkins, S. (2001). *The Universe in a Nutshell*. London: Bantam Press.

HM Treasury (2016). *HM Treasury Analysis: The Immediate Economic Impact of Leaving the EU. Presented to Parliament by the Chancellor of the Exchequer by Command of Her Majesty.* Retrieved from https://www.gov.uk/government/publications/hm-treasury-analysis-the-immediate-economic-impact-of-leaving-the-eu.

Hollander, P. (2016*). From Benito Mussolini to Hugo Chavez: Intellectuals and a Century of Political Hero Worship.* Cambridge: Cambridge University Press.

Höss, R. (1996). *Death dealer: the memoirs of the SS Kommandant at Auschwitz, A. Pollinger (Trans.), S. Paskuly (ed.).* New York: Da Capo Press.

Jarvinen, M. K. and L. Z. Jarvinen, L.Z. (2012). Elevating student potential: Creating digital video to teach neurotransmission. *Journal of Undergraduate Neuroscience Education 11(1)*, ppA6-A7.

Jarvinen, M.K., Jarvinen, L.Z., and Sheehan, D.N. (2012) Application of core science concepts using digital video: A "hands-on" laptop approach. *J. College Science Education 41(6)*, pp. 16-24.

Jobs, S. (1996). *Transcript Extracts of Steve Jobs in conversation with Terry Gross.* Recording available at: https://www.npr.org/2011/10/06/141115121/steve-jobs-computer-science-is-a-liberal-art?t=1571911701235

Jobs, S. (2011). *Transcript of Steve Jobs Speaking at the Apple iPad2 Launch Event.* Created from YouTube video https://www.youtube.com/watch?v=AZeOhnTuq2I.

Johansen, D. (1950). The Integrative Method of Teaching. *The American Journal of Nursing, 50(2)*, pp. 117-119.

Johnson, T.H. (*Ed.*) (1960) . *The Complete Poems of Emily Dickinson.* Boston: Little Brown & Co.

Kahn, D. (1984). Cryptology and the Origins of Spread Spectrum. *IEEE Spectrum, September.* pp. 70-80.

Kahnenman, D. (2011). *Thinking, Fast and Slow.* London: Penguin Books.

Kandel, E.R. (2012). *The Age of Insight: The Quest to Understand the Unconscious in Art, Mind and Brain from Vienna 1900 to the Present.* New York: Random House.

Kandel, E.R. (2016). *Reductionism in Art and Brain Science: Bridging the Two Cultures.* New York: Columbia Univ. Press.

Kasher, S. (1992). The Art of Hitler. *October, 59*, pp. 48-85

Koestler, A. (1989). *The Sleepwalkers: A History of Man's Changing Vision of the Universe.* London: Arkana, Penguin Books. (*Originally published in 1959*).

Kris, E. (1953). *Psychoanalytic Explorations in Art.* London: George Allen & Unwin Ltd.

Kris, E. and Kurz, O. (1979). *Legend, Myth and Magic in the Image of the Artist: A Historical Experiment (A. Laing, Trans.).* New Haven: Yale Univeristy Press. (*Originally published in German in 1934*).

Lawrence, P.A. (2007) The mismeasurement of science. *Current Biology 17(15)*, pp R583-R585

LaMore, R., Root-Bernstein, R., Root-Bernstein, M., Schweitzer, J.H., Lawton, J.L., Roraback, E., Peruski, A., VanDyke, M. and Fernandez, L. (2013). Arts and Crafts: Critical to Economic Innovation. *Economic Development Quarterly 27(3)*, pp. 221-229.

Leighton, S. and Mitchell, P. (Eds.) (2015). *A New STEAM Age: Challenging the STEM Agenda in Research*. London: The Culture Capital Exchange.

Levelt, W. J. M., Drenth, P. and Noort, E. (eds.) (2012). *Flawed Science: The Fraudulent Research Practices of Social Psychologist Diederik Stapel*. Tilburg Univ. Retrieved from: https://www.tilburguniversity.edu/upload/3ff904d7-547b-40ae-85fe-bea38e05a34a_Final%20report%20Flawed%20Science.pdf

MacCurdy, E. (1955). *The Notebooks of Leonardo da Vinci*. New York: George Braziller. (*Originally published in 1939*).

Markey, H.K. and Antheil, G. (1942). *Secret Communication System*. US Patent No. 2,292,387.

Matarasso, F. (2005). *How the Light Gets In: The Value of Imperfect Systems of Cultural Evaluation*. Retrieved from https://parliamentofdreams.files.wordpress.com/2012/05/2005-how-the-light-gets-in-matarasso.pdf.

National Academies of Sciences, Engineering, and Medicine (2016). *National Academies of Sciences Study: Integrating Higher Education in the Arts, Humanities, Sciences, Engineering, and Medicine, Program Book for the Committee Meeting held July 2016 - document pga_175504.pdf:* Retrieved from sites.nationalacademies.org/cs/groups/pgasite/documents/webpage/pga_175504.pdf

National Academies of Sciences, Engineering, and Medicine (2017b). *Fostering Integrity in Research*. Washington, DC: The National Academies Press. Retrieved from https://www.nap.edu/catalog/21896/fostering-integrity-in-research.

National Academies of Sciences, Engineering, and Medicine (2018a). *The Integration of the Humanities and Arts with Sciences, Engineering, and Medicine in Higher Education: Branches from the Same Tree*. Washington, DC: The National Academies Press. Retrieved from https://www.nap.edu/catalog/24988/the-integration-of-the-humanities-and-arts-with-sciences-engineering-and-medicine-in-higher-education

National Academies of Sciences, Engineering, and Medicine (2018b). *Collaborations of Consequence: NAKFI's 15 Years Igniting Innovation at the Intersections of Disciplines*. Washington, DC: The National Academies Press. Retrieved from https://www.nap.edu/catalog/25239/collaborations-of-consequence-nakfis-15-years-igniting-innovation-at-the

National Academies of Sciences, Engineering, and Medicine (2018c). *Graduate STEM Education for the 21st Century*. Washington, DC: The National Academies Press. Retrieved from https://www.nap.edu/catalog/25038/graduate-stem-education-for-the-21st-century

National Endowment for the Arts (2015). *Survey of Public Participation in the Arts, 1982-2008 [United States] – Codebook for 1982 Data*. Ann Arbor, MI: Inter-university Consortium for Political and Social Research [distributor]. Retrieved from: https://www.icpsr.umich.edu/icpsrweb/NADAC/studies/35527/versions/V1/download Doc/doc?path=/pcms/studies/0/3/5/5/35527/V1

National Science Foundation (2009). *Impact of transformative interdisciplinary research and graduate education on academic institutions*. Retrieved from https://www.nsf.gov/pubs/2009/nsf0933/igert_workshop08.pdf

National Survey of Student Engagement. (2011). *Fostering student engagement campuswide – annual results 2011*. Bloomington, IN: Indiana University Center for Postsecondary Research. Retrieved from: http://nsse.indiana.edu/NSSE_2011_Results/pdf/NSSE_2011_AnnualResults.pdf

National Survey of Student Engagement. (2017). *Engagement Insights: Survey Findings on the Quality of Undergraduate Education – Annual Results 2017*. Bloomington, IN: Indiana University Center for Postsecondary Research. Retrieved from http://nsse.indiana.edu/NSSE_2017_Results/pdf/NSSE_2017_Annual_Results.pdf

Nobel Organisation Web Site (n.d.). *The Nobel Prize for Literature 1970*. Retrieved from: https://www.nobelprize.org/prizes/literature/1970/summary/

Norman, D. (26 November 2010). *Why Design Education Must Change*. Retrieved from http://www.idemployee.id.tue.nl/g.w.m.rauterberg/lecturenotes/DG000%20DRP-R/references/norman-2010.pdf

Nowotny, H., Scott, P. and Gibbons, M. (2001). *Re-Thinking Science: Knowledge and the Public in an Age of Uncertainty*. Cambridge: Polity Press.

Olds, B. M. and Miller, R.L. (2004). The effect of a first-year integrated engineering curriculum on graduation rates and student satisfaction: A longitudinal study. *Journal of Engineering Education 93(1)*, pp. 23-35.

O'Reilly, K. (2009). For interdisciplinarity and a disciplined, professional sociology. *Innovation – The European Journal of Social Science Research 22(2)*, pp. 219–32

Ousager, J., and H. Johannessen. 2010. Humanities in undergraduate medical education: A literature review. *Academic Medicine, 85(6)*, pp. 988-998.

Park, H. et.al (2016). Teachers' Perceptions and Practices of STEAM Education in South Korea. *Eurasia Journal of Mathematics, Science & Technology Education, 12(7)*, pp. 1739-1753

Parliamentary Office for Science and Technology (2017). *Research Integrity*. POSTnote POST-PN-0544. Retrieved from http://researchbriefings.parliament.uk/ResearchBriefing/Summary/POST-PN-0544

PCAST STEM Undergraduate Working Group (2012). *Engage to Excel: Producing One Million Additional College Graduates with Degrees in Science, Technology, Engineering, and Mathematics*. Gates, S.J. Jr., Handelsman, J., Lepage, G.P., and Mirkin, C. (eds.). Washington DC: Office of the President.

Philips Design Amsterdam (8 December 2017). *Our People and Places*. Retrieved from https://www.90yearsofdesign.philips.com/our-people-and-places.

Pomeroy, S.R. (2012). *From STEM to STEAM: Science and Art Go Hand-in-Hand*. Retrieved from https://blogs.scientificamerican.com/guest-blog/from-stem-to-steam-science-and-the-arts-go-hand-in-hand/

Psychology Research and Reference (2018). *Motivated Reasoning*. Retrieved from http://psychology.iresearchnet.com/social-psychology/attitudes/motivated-reasoning/

Root-Bernstein, R., *et al.* (2008). Art Fosters Scientific Success: Avocations of Nobel, National Academy, Royal Society and Sigma Xi Members. *J. of Psychology of Science and Technology 1(2)*, pp. 51-63.

Royal Society (2007). *List of Fellows of the Royal Society 1660 – 2007*. Retrieved from https://royalsociety.org/~/media/Royal_Society_Content/about-us/fellowship/Fellows1660-2007.pdf

Sala, G. and Gobet, F. (2017). Does far transfer exist? Negative evidence from chess, music and working memory training. *Current Directions in Psychological Science, 26(6)*, pp. 515-520.

Sapsed, J. andNightingale. P. (2013). *The Brighton fuse report*. Retrieved from: http://www.brightonfuse.com/wp-content/uploads/2013/10/The-Brighton-Fuse-Final-Report.pdf

Shen, J., Jiang, S. and Liu, O. L. (2015). Reconceptualizing a college science learning experience in the new digital era: A review of literature. In: X. Ge, D. Ifenthaler, and J. M. Spector (eds.), *Emerging Technologies for STEAM Education: Full Steam Ahead* (pp. 61-79). Cham, Switzerland: Springer.

Schiuma, G. and Carlucci, D. (2016). Assessing the business impact of arts-based initiatives. In: U. Johansson Sköldberg, J. Woodilla and A. Berthoin Antal (eds.), *Artistic Interventions in Organizations* (pp. 60-73). Abingdon: Routledge.

Scholtz, R.A. (1982). The Origins of Spread-Spectrum Communications. *IEEE Transactions on Communications, Com-30(5)*, pp. 822-584.

Sigma Xi (n.d.). *Becoming a Member*. Retrieved from https://www.sigmaxi.org/members/becoming-a-member

Simon, F. (2014). *EU Twisting Facts to fit Political Agenda, Chief Scientist Says*. Retrieved from http://www.euractiv.com/section/science-policymaking/news/eu-twisting-facts-to-fit-political-agenda-chief-scientist-says/

Snow, C. P. (1956). The Two Cultures. *New Statesman*, 6 October.

Snow, C.P. (1961). *Science and Government*. London: Oxford Univ. Press.

Snow, C.P. (1964). *The Two Cultures and a Second Look: An Expanded Version of the Two Cultures and the Scientific Revolution*. Cambridge: Cambridge Univ. Press.

Snow, C.P. (1965). *The Search*. Harmondsworth: Penguin Books. (*Originally published in 1934*).

Social Theory Rewired (2016). *Habitus – Pierr Bourdieu*. Retrieved from http://routledgesoc.com/category/profile-tags/habitus.

Solzhenitsyn, A. (1972). *Text of Nobel Prize Speech*. Retrieved from: https://www.solzhenitsyncenter.org/nobel-lecture/

Stanford Computer Graphics Laboratory (2013). *The Stanford CityBlock Project: Multi-perspective Panoramas of City Blocks*. Retrieved from http://graphics.stanford.edu/projects/cityblock/

Stentoft, D. (2017). From saying to doing interdisciplinary learning: Is problem-based learning the answer? *Active Learning in Higher Education 18(1)*, pp. 51-61.

Stolk, J.D. and Martello, R. (2015). Can disciplinary integration promote students' lifelong learning attitudes and skills in project-based engineering courses? *International Journal of Engineering Education 31(1B)*, pp. 434-449.

Strengers, Y. A. A. (2014). Interdisciplinarity and industry collaboration in doctoral candidature: Tensions within and between discourses. *Studies in Higher Education 39(4)*, pp. 546-559.

Strickland, E. (2018). Making Medical AI Trustworthy. *IEEE Spectrum, August, pp 8-9.*

Szilard, L. (1948). *The Mark Gable Foundation*. Retrieved from https://library.ucsd.edu/dc/object/bb33804055

Taylor, F.W. (1907). On the Art of Cutting Metals. *Trans. ASME 28*, pp. 31-350.

TEDx Talks (9 May 2017). *Beauty will save the world | Shane Brown | TEDxTwinFalls*. Available at: https://www.youtube.com/watch?v=46Z4tL1ZiuQ

Tavares, J. and Sacco, P. (2015). *Report on the STARTS Symposium in BOZAR, Brussels 22-23 June*. Retrieved from http://www.cheshirehenbury.com/ict-art-connect/ict-art-pdf-files/Report%20on%20Bozar%20Symposium%20June%202015.pdf.

The Economist (2013). *Unreliable Research: Trouble at the Lab. Scientists like to think of science as self-correcting. To an alarming degree, it is not.* Retrieved from https://www.economist.com/news/briefing/21588057-scientists-think-science-self-correcting-alarming-degree-it-not-trouble.

The New York Times (20 March 2011). *Room for Debate – Career Counselor: Bill Gates or Steve Jobs?* Retrieved from: https://www.nytimes.com/roomfordebate/2011/03/20/career-counselor-bill-gates-or-steve-jobs

Touraine, A. (1974). *The Post-industrial Society. Tomorrow's Social History: Classes, Conflicts and Culture in the Programmed Society (Trans. L.F.X. Mayhew)*. London: Wildwood House. (*Originally published in French in 1969*).

Vasari, G. (1898). *Lives of the Most Eminent Painters, Sculptors, and Architects Vol. II (J. Foster, Trans.)*. London. George Bell & Co. (*Originally published 1568*).

Wadhwa, V. (August 3, 2011*). Look at the Leaders of Silicon Valley*. The New York Times. Retrieved from: https://www.nytimes.com/roomfordebate/2011/03/20/career-counselor-bill-gates-or-steve-jobs/look-at-the-leaders-of-silicon-valley

Wadhwa, V., Freeman, R. and Rissing, B. (2008). *Education and Tech Entrepreneurship*. Ewing Marion Kauffman Foundation. Retrieved from: https://www.kauffman.org/-/media/kauffman_org/research-reports-and-covers/2008/06/education_tech_ent_061108.pdf

Wasserstein, R. L., and Lazar, N.A. (2016). The ASA's Statement on p-Values: Context, Process, and Purpose. *The American Statistician 70(2)*, pp.129-133.

Werckmeister, O.K. (1997). Hitler the Artist. *Critical Inquiry, 23(2)*, pp. 270-297

Whewell, W. (1840). *The Philosophy of the Inductive Sciences Founded upon their History. Vol. I.* London: John W. Parker.

Whewell, W. (1848). *The Philosophy of the Inductive Sciences Founded upon their History. Vol. II.* London: John W. Parker.

Whitehead, A.N. (1927). *Science and the Modern World.* Cambridge: Cambridge Univ. Press.

Whitney, J. (1980). *Digital Harmony: On the Complementarity of Music and Visual Art.* Peterborough, NH: Byte Books.

Wikipedia (11 February 2019). *Torpedo.* Retrieved from:
https://en.wikipedia.org/wiki/Torpedo#World_War_II

Wilson, E.O. (1999). *Consilience: The Unity of Knowledge.* London: Abacus.

Wilson, S. (2000). *Myths and Confusions in Thinking about Art/Science/Technology.* Retrieved from http://userwww.sfsu.edu/swilson/papers/wilson.caapaper.html.

Yeats, W.B. (1934). *The Collected Poems of W.B. Yeats.* London: MacMillan & Co. Ltd.

Zhang, D. and Shen, J. (2015). Disciplinary foundations for solving interdisciplinary scientific problems. *International Journal of Science Education 37(15)*, pp. 2555-2576.

www.ingramcontent.com/pod-product-compliance
Lightning Source LLC
Chambersburg PA
CBHW071413090426
42737CB00011B/1451